The material in this book was first presented at the eighth annual women's lectureship of the University Avenue Church of Christ in Denver, Colorado. The same series was enlarged and presented again at the Abilene Christian College lectureship in 1967. In various form these lectures were given to numerous church groups in the Houston area.

THE AUTHOR

Bobbie Lee Holley is mother of four children and wife of Dr. Ed. Holley, Director of Libraries at the University of Houston. She is a *magna cum laude* graduate in English of David Lipscomb College and has an M.A. in English from Northwestern University.

If You Are Interested In . . .

—developing a more meaningful,
   personal relationship in your marriage

—overcoming feelings of loneliness and insecurity

—sharing your children's secrets

—getting more out of church than
   an uncomfortable pew

—having more friends

—gaining a greater
   understanding of God . . .

Then Read This Book!

PERSON TO PERSON

Person to Person

BOBBIE LEE HOLLEY

S SWEET PUBLISHING CO.

AUSTIN   TEXAS

Acknowledgment is gratefully made to
The Macmillan Company for granting permission
to quote "The Leaden-Eyed," by Vachel Lindsay
from *Selected Poems of Vachel Lindsay*, ed. Mark Harris
Copyright 1914 by The Macmillan Company
renewed 1942 by Elizabeth C. Lindsay

Library of Congress Catalog Card Number:78-77236
Standard Book Number: 8344-0005-7

For Ed, rarest husband of them all,
who lovingly accepts me as I am even when I
sit at the typewriter oblivious to both him and
the sink full of dirty dishes

CONTENTS

PREFACE

For some time I have been impressed with the need for more personal communication and understanding in an impersonal world. Counseling with students and friends brought me to the conviction that meaningful person-to-person relationships is one of the major needs of our time.

The material in this book was first presented at the eighth annual women's lectureship of the University Avenue Church of Christ in Denver, Colorado. The same series was repeated at the Abilene Christian College lectureship in 1967. In various form these lectures have also been given before several church groups in the Houston area.

Now, at the urging of several who heard them originally, they are here presented to a larger audience. Some revisions have been made, but essentially they are the same six lectures first presented in Denver.

ACKNOWLEDGMENTS

The ideas and feelings expressed in this book were conceived in the warmth and joy of human relationships and have been "aborning" for many years. It would be impossible to identify all those who through their love, trust and guidance have helped me on the road to becoming a person. I can only say with the poet "I am a part of all that I have met."

How grateful I am to Louise Weirick of Denver, who was willing to risk inviting an "unknown" to speak for the women's lectureship and for the heartfelt responses of the ladies who were in attendance both in Denver and Abilene. Many were kind enough to suggest publication. Mary Lou Walden, who has shared "person to person" over so many years, suggested my name to the lectureship committee at Abilene Christian College, shared her apartment and looked after our youngest child while I was there, and loyally and unfailingly continues to give meaning to the ideas expressed here. Then there are the ladies in my own home congregation who initially listened to my rather tenuous and nebulous ideas. Their suggestions often gave direction to my thoughts and helped me to clarify them.

Rare is the person who responds in love and understanding to the needs of the hour! Doris Arrington, Marie Banister, Reba Bonner, Carolyn Campbell, Verda Farrier, Betty Hudson, Ruth Loney, Arleah Lott, Blynn McGrath, Marion Murray, Sylvia Richards, Jill Shaw and others expressed friendship in so many tangible ways during the days of writing, speaking and revising for publication. They kept the children, often reduced the ironing stack, came by with a salad or dessert for dinner, refrained from dialing my telephone number, encouraged me and believed in the value of what I was doing, lifted me up in prayer, and by the very beauty of their lives provided subject matter and inspiration. The children—Gailon, Jens, Amy and Beth—have been cooperative in their chores most of the time and have respected study times. Mrs. Iris Williams and Miss Sue Greenwood were certainly helpful with many of the typing chores.

Husbands are by no means a rarity, but I rather think that husbands who cheer their wives on in madness and indulge them in faithlessness to at least the lesser household chores were never a prolific breed. Ed, unperturbed by such, has provided the practical, emotional and spiritual help necessary not only for writing books but also for living each day.

Other than Ed and the children, my friend Buzzie Ball has no doubt suffered most of all. She has read or heard every word a dozen times or more. She has walked with me in the valleys of despair and on the mountains of optimism. She's prayed with me, listened to me think aloud, helped me find references, offered concrete suggestions and taken me away when my mind was too tired to function further. She'd often breeze in, run the sweeper, iron a shirt or two, fold the clothes and be on her way. Thank you, Buzzie, for all this but more for the light of love and God that has flooded my life because of you and for giving substance to the very idea of person-to-person relationships.

Bobbie Lee Holley
Houston, Texas

Chapter One

Touching Wounds

UP THE DOWN STAIRCASE is a novel that concerns a newly-minted teacher whose first assignment was in one of the high schools in metropolitan New York. Sylvia was idealistic; she wanted to get through to her students. She cared, she was concerned about their lives. Because she had the slow learners, the non-achievers, the ones who couldn't read, the ones who were waiting to reach the dropout age, she didn't really have much hope of teaching them "English," but she sincerely wanted to make a difference in their lives, to touch them in a way that would help them to live in the chaotic circumstances in which they found themselves. But she was frustrated on every hand. The other teachers felt nothing any more; she was swamped with the "red tape" of administration and hampered by the rules.

She began to write of her experiences to her friend. In one of the first letters she told Ellen of the girl who had asked to see her after school. Because it was faculty conference day, Sylvia had to refuse her. Absence from the sacred gathering was inexcusable. Now the truant officer had reported that she had run away. Sylvia couldn't help thinking that she might have been able to help her.

Two weeks later she wrote to the same friend:

"Evelyn Lazar is dead. That's the girl who asked to see me the day of the Faculty Conference. Perhaps if I had, she would be alive today. She died of an infection following an abortion she had tried to induce with a knitting needle, after she had run away from home. Now she's but a name to be removed from the home-room register. Permanently."[1]

Then she relates the reactions of various teachers to the incident:[2]

"Think only of yourself. Getting involved does them no good."

"You're not God. Nothing is your fault, except, perhaps, poor teaching."

"If you've kept them off the streets and given them a bit of fun for a while, you've earned your keep...."

One—her only real friend among the faculty— "spoke of love; that's what these children were starved for." Another made fun of this and said that they couldn't handle love because they knew nothing about it and added that "amused detachment is the only way to remain intact." Another suggested, "I started out like you, too, but I found there's nothing you can do, so you may as well give up." One teacher said coldly: "Sterilize them and kick them out of school."

The school nurse, trying to allay Sylvia's feelings, suggested that nothing could have been done. She knew something of Evelyn's home life and troubles with her father. She told Sylvia that she had given Evelyn a cup of tea one morning when she came in beaten black and blue. Incensed, Sylvia demanded to know what help a cup of tea could possibly be. Angrily, the nurse pointed out that she had begged, pleaded, banged on her desk to get some responsible group or individual to understand about the deplorable lives of the kids and to do something for them. Nobody listened and she was forbidden to give them even so much as an adhesive bandage. She showed Sylvia the directive from the school board posted on her wall: "THE SCHOOL NURSE MAY NOT TOUCH WOUNDS, GIVE MEDICATION, REMOVE FOREIGN PARTICLES FROM THE EYE...."[3]

None of us wants to touch wounds, and this is the condition of our society that seems constantly to confront us in the newspapers, magazine articles, religious journals, sociology textbooks, modern art, drama and literature. Call it many things: the "lonely crowd," the depersonalization of individuals, secularization, the lack of concern and care, detachment from the lives of others. T. S. Eliot wrote, "No man knows or cares who his neighbor is, unless his neighbor makes too much disturbance."[4] It is not difficult to relate example after example.

Not long ago a study was made of a group of girls who had married quite young and, for the most, quite unwisely. These girls were not from the lower social and economic levels as one might expect but from the substantial middle class. Most of them were church members and had a fairly regular pattern of attendance, but almost all of them said that they had gone to large, urban, impersonal churches and felt that they had no one with whom to talk.

In the state of New Jersey during a three-year period (1961-1963) 41 children around the age of 15 committed suicide, and another 738 attempted to do so. Not one of them had a confidant of any age to whom he or she could communicate his personal distress. Here were children desperate to be loved, to be accepted and to be heard; but there was no one.

Many older persons sit in frustration and loneliness as the endless hours go by. Our mental hospitals are overflowing with people who live in isolated worlds of their own because they have been deprived of meaningful relationships until they are no longer capable of contact. Alcoholism is a major national problem, and we are told that many drift into this escape world because the real world is too painful for them. They have ceased to be real persons. Nobody cares. Nobody "touches the wounds."

In the church I feel a growing insensitivity to persons. It is so easy for an impersonal atmosphere to develop. We speak to people on Sunday mornings, ask about their jobs or their children or some church project—but do we really know how our fellow Christians think, what they feel, what their problems are, what they strive for, what burdens they carry? Do we know enough to clasp a hand, look deeply into another's eyes and communicate a sense of deep understanding and love with perhaps no words being spoken at all?

People are lonely. Individuals are crying out for deep understanding, for someone to listen, for a sense of acceptance in all their weakness and frustration. I have found that often the most sophisticated, the most seemingly poised and secure, those who seem most completely to have conquered themselves and their world, are the hungriest. So many times—especially in the church—those who seem sinless, who sound the holiest, who do the most "good things" are inwardly ashamed of themselves, their sins, their inadequacies; but they can't admit it because they have an "image" to preserve. They can't communicate their fright and guilt and confusion because the other people in the church look so happy and committed and peaceful that they don't have the courage to admit their own deep needs.

A teacher-training class that I recently taught turned out to be one of the most exciting experiences I have ever had. I'm sure that anyone walking into the class during some of our sessions would have wondered what relation our discussions could possibly have to teaching. What was really happening was that we were discovering ourselves; and as I see the teaching life, there is no more important quality for the Christian teacher than that she be an authentic person, a *real* person, one who faces her own strengths and weaknesses honestly, who knows her own worth, and who sustains a very real and living relationship with God.

The importance of these class sessions lay in the fact that the barriers that shut us off from each other were being slowly eliminated; we were revealing our inmost feelings without shame or embarrassment and with complete trust in each other. One of the members, a rather shy, withdrawn person, said later, "I didn't dream that those people could possibly have the same problems and questions and misgivings that I do. I thought I was the only one who felt this way." She particularly mentioned one of the younger women. "I couldn't have believed that she needed anybody." She was referring to a young mother—beautiful and sophisticated—seemingly poised and with all the confidence to meet any situation. We often look at persons like this and think that they stand alone and sure, self-contained and fulfilled. I don't understand why but we especially seem to feel this way about lovely, well-dressed, "society-type" women. We seem not to realize that someone like this wants or needs sensitive understanding by others or a deep spiritual life. Nothing could be further from the truth. This young mother feels deep needs and longings, she wants to be a good mother, she wants a vital life with God. She wanted someone to listen.

Keith Miller in his book *The Taste of New Wine* tells a similar story. A young party-type mother, whose actions were often shocking, had come to his prayer and discussion group, despairing and desperate, on the brink of divorce. She was a church member, but she felt a need for something that she didn't have. She found in this group understanding and acceptance and a peace that she had never known. Weeks later she very quietly said to the group,

> You know, all of my life I've been trying to get your attention, I have showed off, told risque stories, and done all kinds of things to get you to notice me, to love me.... And when you didn't I gossiped about you, cut you to ribbons behind your backs, because I was miserable. I wanted to be something; I wanted so much to be something in your eyes.[5]

A sensitive article by Philip Dunning, entitled "Every Fellow Needs a Friend," relates the story of a little boy who wandered off the street into a certain Sunday school. He started attending regularly but became a real troublemaker. He was insolent and argumentative. He bullied the other children. When the teacher went to the director, she saw only two choices: get rid of him or get rid of me. His reply was, "Now, Mrs. Smith, I know that Butch is a problem, but don't you think the church ought to be helping him—not throwing him out." He knew that Butch's parents were alcoholics and his sister a prostitute. When he talked with him, Butch sobbed, "Nobody

likes me—why should I care if I do anything right?...
I never want to even go home again." Because someone cared enough to listen, a real friendship grew between a troubled boy who needed a friend and a man who was willing to be a friend.[6]

Young people need friends—someone to listen to them—whether or not they're in trouble. In my years of teaching both in a small church-related high school and in a large public high school, I found that the teacher who is available and genuinely concerned always has afternoon visitors.

Recently a friend of mine became the teacher for a group of ninth grade girls in our church community. Some of the students have said openly that this is the most meaningful class they've ever had because there is an atmosphere of freedom and acceptance and love that makes it possible for them to acknowledge their feelings and ask questions without fear of being rejected and condemned. My friend has been amazed at the way the students seek her out, stop her in the halls, wait to walk with her after class, spot her after worship and rush across the room to her to say something. They have perceived in her an understanding friend. They want to be with her and find the merest excuses to do so. Already she means a great deal to these young girls because she genuinely cares about them.

Two of my closest and dearest friends are women who seemed to me when I first knew them not to need anyone. They were surrounded by friends; people were in and out of their houses all the time. They were in bridge clubs, they were busy in "church activities." One of them told me recently—and this is several years later—"All of my life I've longed for someone to talk to as I can to you." It isn't easy for any of us to let others into the most sacred recesses of our lives—and in this I feel that we so often rob one another of great beauty and blessing.

Yes, people are lonely and every fellow needs a friend. It is in personal relationships that individual lives are formed, deformed or transformed.

But, you are apt to say, what else can we do? We're busy. We serve on community projects, we give our time to lots of church activities, and we do have our families. This is true, and these responsibilities are important; but what I'm really afraid of is that many of us hide behind the impersonal nature of some of these projects because person-to-person relationships are much more difficult to achieve and much more costly to ourselves. It is dangerous and demanding to become involved in others' lives.

Person-to-person relationships! Paul and Jesus talked about them so much: "pray one for another," "confess your sins one to another," "love one another," "exhort one another," "comfort one another," "bear one another's burdens." But what does this really mean? Don't we have person-to-person relationships all the time? No, we don't. To be sure, we're with people all the time—surrounded with them. But "person to person" doesn't mean just "face to face." Perhaps "heart to heart" would express it more meaningfully. It doesn't mean just helping people. Help can insult, estrange, and separate. It means meeting people on the inside, at the point of their real selves. It means listening to unspoken needs, cries for help, appeals for friendship, love, understanding and acceptance. It means recognizing the essential qualities of people—whatever it is that makes them personalities, unique and different. It means giving them the freedom to be themselves, to be what God meant them to be. It means touching the wounds no matter how ugly, how distasteful, how frightening. It also means sharing the most cherished parts of life: joy, happiness, accomplishment, ideas, faith, the depths of our own beings.

How do we build person-to-person relationships? What are the characteristics?

THE VALUE OF OTHERS

It seems to me that at the very heart of person-to-person relationships is the ability to look upon each person as being of value and worth, as having something of the "image of God" in him no matter what his successes or failures or problems or goals may be. No matter how far away from our own standards and ideals he may be, he must be taken seriously; and he must be accepted for just what he is and made to feel as if he is a person, important in his own right.

This is not easy to do; there seems to be a deep-seated desire in almost all of us to manipulate people. We want our children, our husbands, our friends to go where we want them to go, to be what we want them to be. We think we have the answers for other persons' lives. We judge and condemn. How often do you reject others, perhaps in very subtle ways? We even rebuff people on the basis of the kind of clothes they wear. I have been in women's gatherings where the whole conversation centered on others' lack of taste in clothes and hair styles. I even know of one situation where one man asked that a minister be dismissed because he didn't like the clothes he wore. For trifling details we reject those whose lives might have much to offer us. Recently a friend wrote me a note and said, "I don't feel that you are concerned with the way I stand or dress or comb my hair—but you are concerned about my joy and pain...."

Bonhoeffer speaks effectively of how we should feel when we look at any person:

> God did not make this person as I would have made him. He did not give him to me ... for me to dominate and control, but in order that I might find above him the Creator.... God does not will that I should fashion the other person according to the image that seems good to me, that is, in my own image; rather in his very freedom from me God made this person in His image. I can never know beforehand how God's image should appear in others. That image always manifests a completely new and unique form that comes solely from God's free and sovereign creation. To me the sight may seem strange, even ungodly. But God creates every man in the likeness of His Son, the Crucified.[7]

It is not ours to fashion but to help people to be what God intends them to be. This we can do only through acceptance, understanding and permitting. It is only as persons are free to be themselves that they can accept themselves and then be free to change in desirable ways.

Included in the idea of allowing others to be themselves is the idea of permitting them to make their own decisions. I think one of the most presumptive actions we can undertake is to tell another person how to run his life, how he should live, what choices he should make. Do you remember Job and his friends? I'm sure that he received a great deal of comfort as long as they were sitting quietly with him, but then they decided that it was incumbent upon them to set him straight. They knew just exactly what was wrong with him and what he should do about it. What they failed to understand was that Job had to find the way for himself. Even if they had been right, he was not ready to receive their answers. If we truly believe in people, believe that persons have the ability to move toward the positive and mature, then we will not want to fix things, to set goals, to mold people, to manipulate them and to push them in pre-determined ways.

Back to *Up the Down Staircase*: one boy in Sylvia's class was among the slowest learners. He felt no identity. He said that nobody ever remembered his name; he was "nobody" and he wouldn't even sign his name on his papers. He just put "me." But the teacher gave him one experience in class that really made a difference in his life. He was somebody that day—for the first time ever. Later he wrote her a note: "I, for one, will never forget you as long as I live. You made me feel I'm real."[8] He signed his name. She had made him feel as if he were worth something.

In a small rural church in Illinois, where my husband often drove on Sundays to preach when we lived in that part of the country, there was a lovely lady whose home became a haven for us. The friendship she offered us—including our children who were then quite small—was warm and beautiful. Even though we often had dinner and spent Sunday afternoons with her, she never went to Sunday evening services with us. She never offered any explanation and we, of course, never asked any questions. One day we found out why she didn't come. We were a bit later than usual getting away on that Sunday evening; and before we left, an elderly lady had come to her door. She was frail and a bit stooped and somehow one's heart went out to her without thinking of a reason. We were introduced and our family went our way. Later we learned something further. This was her friend—a widow in very poor health and with few financial resources. She lived in a dingy little room and had very few, if any, who cared for her. Each Sunday evening our friend invited this widow to her home, fixed dinner for her, and spent several hours talking, sharing, making her feel loved and important. One lonely little person being reached out to by another who understood!

Don't you like to feel as if someone cares for you, accepts you just as you are so that you don't have to pretend, is glad when you walk into the room? I do; I couldn't live without it. Sometimes one of my children will burst through the door and say, "Look who's here, Mom!" In effect he is responding to his own faith that I, his mother, will respond to him as a person—an important person.

LEARNING TO LISTEN

Person-to-person relationships cannot be built until we have learned to listen to each other. How often do we really listen to people—our husbands, our children, our friends—with no other thought in mind than just trying to hear and understand what they are really saying and to feel the emotions enveloping the words? There is a young person in my congregation who has far more problems than one so young should be burdened with. She comes sometimes to talk with me. One night after she had said something she looked at me and said, "What are you thinking?"

By this question she was seeking to determine if I were passing judgment on her. When I answered that I was not thinking anything but was trying to understand what she was saying to me, her reply was, "It's unusual for anybody to care what I'm saying." Have you ever noticed that when we are engaged in conversation, so much of the time we are thinking of what we want to say and trying to find a moment when we can interrupt to say it instead of really listening? Sometimes one of my children will say, "Mother, you're not listening to me." And I really won't be.

Listening is an activity that requires discipline, unusual alertness and gentleness. It is not at all the inertia we often make of it. A listener must hear not only the spoken words but the nuances of meaning and emotional involvement of the speaker, the unspoken, the signs of address. In turn, the other person must know that he has been heard and understood. Listening and understanding do not imply agreement or acceptance of the speaker's views but rather an openness to him and respect for his feelings and thoughts. True listening requires an open heart as well as open ears. When we truly listen to another, we affirm our belief in his dignity, his freedom, and his reliability.

All of us want to be listened to. Seneca voiced this yearning long ago:

> For who listens to us in all the world, whether he be friend, or teacher, brother or father or mother, sister or neighbor, son or servant? Does he listen, our advocate, or our husbands or our wives—those who are dearest to us?

> Do the stars listen, when we turn despairingly away from men, or great winds, or the seas or the moun-

tains? To whom can any man say—'Here I am! Behold
me in my nakedness, my wounds, my secret grief, my
despair, my betrayal, my pain, my tongue which cannot express my sorrow, my terror, my abandonment.
Listen to me for a day—an hour—a moment! .... O God,
is there no one to listen?'[9]

The man of Seneca's day seems no different from
contemporary man, for it seems that he does not
really listen.

SENSITIVITY TO OTHERS

Building person to person relationships requires
developing a sensitivity to the needs, the moods, the
feelings of others. It means becoming involved in
the lives of others, and you should know that this
sometimes means getting hurt yourself. It means being able to see and to feel from the inside, to put
yourself in another's place, to live in others' experiences. When we look only from the outside, we are apt
to be cold and critical and unloving. Harry Emerson
Fosdick in *The Meaning of Service* describes Jesus'
fulfillment of the Golden Rule:

> He saw by sympathy the prodigal's problem from with-
> in, when all the Pharisees around were condemning
> him as lost. He saw from within the meaning of the
> widow's slender gift and the passionate outpouring of
> Mary's gratitude is costly oil. He saw from within
> the way life looked to Zacchaeus and from within he
> knew the secret sifting of Peter's soul by Satan. The
> woman taken in adultery, with the crowd of angry men
> around, their robes girt up, and stones in hand to slay
> her—even her problem he saw from within, and per-
> ceived in her what no one looking from without could
> possibly have guessed. ... One must see men as he does
> stained glass in a cathedral window, not from without
> in, but from within out.[10]

I recently read a touching story that so well illustrates the quality of feeling with others. A little girl came home much later than she should have from playing with a friend. Her mother was angry with her and asked impatiently, "Where have you been?"

"Well, Mother, Sally broke her doll."

"What does that have to do with you. You couldn't fix it and that's certainly no excuse for being late!"

"But, Mother, I had to stay and help her cry."

In person-to-person relationships one may often need to stay to help another cry.

BUILDING TRUST

In the next place, there must be a building of trust. Trust between persons does not come overnight. Think of your dearest and closest friends—those whom you trust completely, those with whom you share most deeply. It took time, didn't it? We must be absolutely honest with ourselves and with others if we are to establish the kind of trust that frees people to talk, to release their feelings, to be themselves, to grow. This is so important in all our relationships. We don't confess our sins to one another very often. Isn't it partly because we can't be honest with ourselves and because we can't trust others?

In a class of high school girls that I once taught was one girl who had not responded to any teacher she had ever had. I was told that she was uninterested, uncooperative, and unresponsive to any suggestions. "Just don't let her bother you," one person said. How wrong they were! This girl didn't need lessons on the book of Acts or church doctrine. She didn't even need the lessons on courtship and marriage that I was teaching. She needed one person in the world that she could trust. She needed one person that cared about her. She trusted neither father nor mother—and for good reasons. Nobody looked at her as a person with feelings, with longings, with infinite possibilities. I was thrilled and grateful the first time she called me and said, "I'd like to come over to talk with you." It didn't happen easily; it must have been at least a year before she trusted me enough to talk about the things in her heaped-up heart. A lot has happened to this girl since then. She graduated from a church college and is a devoted Christian. "[Jesus] saw possibilities within people who had been termed hopeless by others, and he believed them into new life."[11] I wonder how often we believe people into new life.

GIVING OUR TIME

The loving gift of time is necessary for authentic and life-giving personal relations. The use of precious and fleeting minutes must be planned in many instances over periods of months or years. You must be unhurried and able to convey to others the feeling that you want to be with them, that you enjoy sharing experiences with them. Once I asked a friend to share what could have been a very enjoyable afternoon for both of us. She refused but later she apologized and said, "I couldn't really believe that you wanted to spend that time with me or that you really cared whether or not I went."

It has been said of the late President John Kennedy that whenever he was with another person, he had the enviable ability to make that person feel that for that space of time he had nothing else to do than experience the *now* with him. Past and future were blotted out as he talked, asked questions and listened intently to what the other had to say. This is an art that can be developed only through sincerity and honest willingness to give time to others. It is true that we often do not have many measurable minutes, and yet for the time we have we can make another feel that there is no other immediate concern than what is important to him. In this way fifteen minutes can be utilized more effectively than an hour of hurried, frantic, distracted, uneasy presence.

There are, of course, occasions that demand brevity as when we visit a very sick person in the hospital or when another is very busy, and we could so easily rob him of much-needed time. On the other hand, there are those who need much time from someone genuinely interested and concerned. It is emotionally draining and time-consuming to become involved in the sorrow of a new widow or with the mother whose son was killed in Vietnam. For the person deeply distressed or depressed it may mean phone calls in the middle of the night. So few are willing to pay the price, to be on call, or to give up more pleasant activities to spend time with those who have needs.

Elton Trueblood suggests in *The Company of the Committed* a rather paradoxical secret for the discipline of time: a fuller date book. If we include in our calendar of daily activities the names of those who need our time, then we would not be so tempted to waste our hours with the shallow and unimportant. At the same time, however, we need to be careful not to fill each day so full that we cannot be interrupted by those with authentic demands or requests.

LOVE IS ESSENTIAL

Finally, all that I have said must be infused with love, must be grounded in and surrounded by love, must flow from love. We must be possessed by love—the unconditional, the *agape* of which Paul speaks in 1 Corinthians 13 and of which John writes in the beautiful language of 1 John. *Agape* is love that asks nothing in return, love that goes out to the unlovely and unappreciative, love that confirms people and sees in them what they can become, love that goes beyond all reason, love that is impractical and extravagant, love that pours out costly ointment and washes feet, love that accomplishes the impossible, forgives the deepest hurts and is finally crucified if necessary.

This is the kind of love described in an old short story in which a small boy was bewitched into killing his mother. He took the heart from her lifeless body to the witch who lived on the hill. The youngster stumbled on the rugged path and dropped the heart. As he reached to pick it up, he thought he heard the heart murmur, "My child, did you hurt yourself?"

Agape is more than just a desire to help, more than just giving, and more than just an emotion. Paul Tillich has suggested, "In mutual assistance what is most important is not the alleviation of need but the actualization of love. Of course, there is no love which does not want to make the other's need its own. But there is also no true help which does not spring from love and create love."[12] It's much easier to offer some kind of tangible assistance than it is to offer love. For instance, we can go "slumming" and offer food and clothes and feel very content with our good deeds; but that's far different from building helping relationships. In addition to seeking to make the gift equal the need, love adds a dimension which binds heart to heart and life to life.

In Paul's familiar words: "If I have not love, I am nothing" (1 Cor. 13:2). John says, "If we love one another, God abides in us and his love is perfected in us" (I John 4:12).

The life of love has always been costly. To love is to be like Jesus. "Being like Jesus of Nazareth in a world like this is not a prospect to be viewed with composure. To love where love is crucified; to be unselfish where the crowd will take advantage of your unselfishness, cheat you for being honest, and hurt your feelings for showing yourself affectionate."[13]

In the very lovely book, *I and Thou*,[14] Martin Buber describes the two primary relationships on which life is based: "I-Thou" and "I-It." The essence of these responses to life does not depend upon the character of the objects or persons opposite the "I" but rather upon the nature of the relations between them. The "I-It" category concerns the ordered world and a person's use and experience of it. Objects and people exist for his use, for specific purposes, often for calculated benefits. The "I" is absorbed with individuality, appropriation, introspection and "my" rather than with personhood, relationship and sharing. This kind of relating to the world is not necessarily evil; indeed it is necessary, for the reliability of an ordered world sustains us. It is only when one is unwilling to enter into personal relations that life is untransformed and despairing.

"I-Thou" becomes a reality when one turns toward and reaches out to another in openness, directness, intensity and mutuality. He is fully aware of the personality and being of the other, and he responds openly with his whole being to his "otherness," allowing him to exist in his own uniqueness and "specialness." He does not become one with the other person nor does he seek to engulf him or appropriate him into his own personality. Both stand in directness and are able to experience events from both sides of the relationship. Buber sees love as the recognition of the other's freedom, "different-ness," independence and worth. It is the responsibility of an "I" for a "Thou."

Life cannot be lived solely in either of the primary relationships but rather there must be a constant shifting. "I-Thou" must be the foundation underlying the objective relationships. The indirect world of "It" must be brought again and again into the direct meeting with "Thou." "I-Thou" gives meaning and spirit to the world of "It." In the alternating a person remains authentic.

Appreciation, acceptance, listening, confirming, reaching out, sharing, concern, trust, time, self, love—this is the stuff of heart-to-heart relationships. This is the kind of involvement that must characterize every area in which our lives touch the lives—and wounds—of others if there is to be any real vitality or any real Christianity, if people are to become what they are capable of becoming, if they are to find the abundant life.

Man's deepest need is to love and be loved.
But man is lonely,
   because he doesn't feel he can trust his goodness
   and his badness
   to his fellow men.

So he wears a mask of superficial respectability.
He tries to compensate for his loneliness
    by surrounding himself with labor-saving gadgets,
    prestige-producing possessions,
    and attention absorbing amusements.
But to no avail,
    for man is not a thing—he is a person—
    made to respond and be responded to;
    made for interaction and communication
    with other persons and with God.[15]

Chapter Two

Family Give and Take

THE HOME IS ONE of the places where we need to be keenly aware of the need for special attention to person-to-person relationships and very sensitive to their quality. Within the family God has provided for the most personal and intimate interplay of personalities. Here the patterns of life are determined and the destinies of life are realized or defeated. The most beautiful feelings, the deepest communion, the sweetest sharing of plans and hopes, the most creative cooperation and the most complete personality fulfillment should be nurtured here. Yet, this is often the place where the greatest barriers, the deepest antagonisms and fears, the most profound hatreds and rivalries, the most terrible violence done to personality and the greatest distance between hearts are witnessed.

It would seem unnecessary to talk about acceptance and freedom and love in the context of the home, for, of course, we all accept and love our children and our husbands and our parents. How nice it would be if the picture were this pretty! Even our Christian homes do not project so ideal a situation.

Every mother has at times rejected her children. If we're really honest, we have to admit that. For most of us this is a passing experience; and when we acknowledge the feeling, we can usually understand the reasons, confess our emotional weaknesses and reaffirm our love. But in many instances the rejection is not temporary; it is long-lasting and permanently damaging. In a recent television interview, two psychiatrists who operate a home for neglected children told of a little boy who had been forgotten after the birth of another child in the family. Eventually, in his frustration and loneliness, the child killed the baby. His parents, hate-filled and bitter, left him at the home with a note for the officials to take care of him if they could. "We don't love him and God don't love him." Surely this little fellow must have felt utterly and completely rejected, and it is doubtful that anyone would be capable of providing enough love to alleviate the damage he has sustained. Home is about the most important word in the vocabulary of a child. It is his only security; and although it may be a miserable one, he still builds up associations around it—many of them idealized. Even this little boy wanted to go home. People love through life what they loved as children, and perhaps love is the only treasure that can never be taken away.

There was a child in the first grade class with my oldest child whose mother was determined that her son was going to excel. Strictness and perfection were her guidewords; and because she was a friend of the teacher, she urged her to be strict and demanding with him. My son Gailon used to come home and tell me what the teacher had done to the other little boy. I cringed and was so grateful that Gailon was a good student because I didn't think he could take the treatment that the other child was getting, and I was pretty sure I wouldn't stand for it. The more the teacher and the boy's mother nagged and the more they pressured and the more they ridiculed and the more they punished, the worse he became. He did not do well academically, and he developed rather serious nervous problems. Finally they came to realize that he has to grow in his own way and at his own rate, and that he is what he is.

Perhaps most of you know families in which there is a child who is constantly nagged, who can never do anything that pleases, who is never complimented or praised. He is pressured, pressured, pressured to become that which he is not, to be perfect, to be good. The threat that love will be withheld is always lurking in the background. I'm sure that we've all been guilty of a little of this. With such faultfinding a child can't be big or think big because he is always being belittled and cut down.

So often we make fun of or disregard our children's best efforts. The little gifts they bring to you—the tiny crushed flower picked just for you, the smudged valentine or Christmas card—what do you do with them? Do you put the flower in water—even if it's a wild onion? I'll tell you what I do with the pictures, the notes, the valentines: I hang them on my dresser or my bedroom door, and I can assure you that I have the messiest bedroom door in the neighborhood. My husband has the little paperweight that one of the children made for him on his office desk. These are the gifts of their hearts and your rejection of their offerings is to them a rejection of themselves. Soon they'll stop bringing anything to you, including their ideas and thoughts. You may think them foolish or laugh at them or discard them.

The greatest test of our love and care come when the child is unlovely, when he has been ugly, when he has, as an older child, done wrong. It is so very difficult to let the child know that you love him, that he is just as surely in your heart when he is disobedient and rebellious as when he is sweet and cooperative, but at the same time to show disapproval of his behavior or action. If we could only realize that there is a reason for a child's misbehavior, and very often we may be the cause! So often he's trying to tell us something. He may be saying to you, "Look at me, Mother, have you forgotten that I exist, that I'm yours. I need you; I need to know you love me." That's the way it is with my children. Two of them give me very clear and definite warning signs when I become too involved with other things and neglect them. One begins to whine about everything and to cling to me with tears whenever I leave even to go to the grocery store. Another becomes sloppy in his dress, in the keeping of his room, in his schoolwork. He becomes disgruntled and unpleasant and often disobedient and stormy.

After boys and girls get older and make more serious mistakes, parents often just erase their names from the family roster as far as any sympathy or understanding is concerned. I know that parents are often hurt by their children, and it's hard to take. Children are often hurt by parents too. But it seems to me to be the role of love to try to understand the action and feelings of the child and try to help him.

A young girl fell in love with an older married man. Before anyone else knew about it, they had planned to marry as soon as he could secure a divorce. This girl was a sweet girl—pretty, innocent and naive—

who had been carried away by the flattery of the older man who professed that theirs was the love of all ages. Knowing both of them, my husband talked with them; and he was able to help her to see the situation objectively. But her mother was absolutely irrational and hysterical. "What have you done to our family name?" was all that she could shout at her daughter. The girl needed help to work through her problem and to try to understand what had happened in order to understand herself better, but she couldn't talk to her mother. She came to our home many nights to talk and to sound out her thoughts and feelings. One night she said, "I know that you don't approve of this any more than my mother does, but you will let me talk about it and you don't make me feel as if I've suddenly turned to scum."

One day my husband received a telephone call from some friends, asking him to come to the hospital. He went; he returned broken-hearted. Their young daughter had just given birth to an illegitimate child. In the ensuing weeks we were with that family many times, trying to help and be of comfort as we could. The mother, as any of us would be probably, was broken and pathetic and quite unable to cope with the situation. But she did not denounce her daughter or reject her. And that father proved himself to be one of the kindest, most understanding men I have ever known. He did not try to minimize the wrong or to deny it. He was heart-broken too, but he was a tower of emotional and spiritual strength to his daughter and to his wife. His love for her never wavered, and he did everything he could to make it easier for her and to make all arrangements that were necessary. That girl is now happily married to a fine Christian boy who knew of her past and who was willing to accept her and love her as she was—penitent and sorry for what had happened. Had her parents acted differently she might have gone further and further down the path to ruin and degradation.

I think that it is in this particular relationship— that of parent and child—that we have the greatest difficulty in refraining from molding and manipulating. Our own egos get in the way so easily. We want our children to be what we were not able to be. We want to realize our unfulfilled dreams in them. We want the credit and glory of what they become. We want them to reflect our training and our codes. God didn't give them to us as possessions to be grasped unto ourselves. We so often are not able to give ourselves in love and devotion because we are absorbed in ourselves. And so we alienate those with whom we would be closest.

Very closely allied with the idea of acceptance is that of freedom: freedom to grow, freedom to explore, freedom to experiment, freedom to think, freedom to make choices and to suffer the consequences of those choices, freedom to become what God intends them to be. This seems harder to grant as children grow older, and I think that one of the saddest situations I know is that in which a parent and child never have a mature, adult relationship because the parents never let the child grow up.

Sometimes in homes there appears to be a calm, happy surface; yet it is one in which eventually the children are emotional cripples, unfit for the processes of life because they have been so dominated by one or both parents. Havelock Ellis in his book,

On Life and Sex, suggests that in these circumstances

> the parents often take as their moral right the services
> which should only be accepted, if accepted at all, as the
> offering of love and gratitude, and even reach a degree
> of domineering selfishness in which they refuse to be-
> lieve that their children have any adult rights of their
> own, absorbing and drying up that physical and spiri-
> tual life-blood of their offspring which it is the parents'
> part in Nature to feed.... Their time and energy are
> not their own; their tastes are criticised and so far as
> possible crushed; their political ideas, if they have any,
> are treated as pernicious; and—which is often on both
> sides the most painful of all—differences in religious
> belief lead to bitter controversy and humiliating re-
> crimination.[1]

Not only should the parent allow the young spirit
to essay its own wings; but

> if its energy is not equal to the adventure, then it is the
> part of a truly loving parent to push it over the edge
> of the nest.[2]

In one of the schools in which I taught there was a
particular teacher for whom I developed an appreciation and respect. She was an interesting person and
I admired her ability to work so patiently and kindly
with the slow learners and readers. Several times I
asked her to go somewhere with me after school—to
the art gallery once as I remember. I asked her to go
home with me from school one day and stay for dinner. But each time she refused, and the picture became very clear after a while. She lived with a domi-
nating mother, and she had to go directly home from
school. She went nowhere at night alone unless it
was to a required school function. This woman must
have been about forty at that time.

There are many married children whose parents
cannot let them live their own lives. I know of a

young couple who married—each an only child and both from Christian families. In fact, they met at a church school. The parents of those two literally tore that marriage apart; they could not keep hands off. His parents told him how to treat his wife and what to make her do; but at the same time her mother was telling her just what to do.

So often when an older child or young adult expresses an opinion quite different from a belief of the parents, the parents take it as a personal affront. One of the most wonderful Christian couples I know have a son who is an atheist. The father has refused to become an elder in several congregations because of this. I know that their hearts are heavy over this boy, and I also know that they are knowledgeable, devoted, studious, understanding Christian parents. But the thing that impresses me is that they live their lives quietly and devotedly, and they have not erected barriers in their relationship with the son. They do not nag and preach and they listen honestly and sincerely to his views. They don't approve and I know they are anxious for his soul. But they know that only through leaving doors open will he ever come back. They respect his freedom and they can discuss without anger or bitterness. The way we treat our boys and girls during their periods of doubt and experimenting with new ideas and challenging of what they've been taught is extremely important. We must be patient and calm and reassuring and show them by our lives that we have something rare and sure to guide us.

We simply cannot impose our values and beliefs on our children from the outside. Each child must come to his own value system and must be given the opportunity to develop his own if it is to be his guide for all the circumstances of life. I am not saying that we should not teach our children; certainly it is our responsibility to pass on to our children the best we know and the best that we have. There must be teaching, but it must find meaning in experience. There must be goals, but they must be realistic; they must be accepted by the child and they must speak to his needs. The strength of the teaching lies in the strength of the life of the parent and other individuals important in the life of the child.

Children imitate those whom they love and adore. They must find their own lessons in their experiences. They eventually come to the point of making choices after reflective thinking and analysis of various situations and we have to give them freedom to make their own mistakes sometimes. I believe that it is precisely for this reason that we find much of the rebellion among young people. They have not been allowed to develop through many experiences their own conscience and system of behavior, but parental codes have been placed upon them arbitrarily and often unlovingly. When all of this is said, perhaps the most important understanding is that values are more caught than taught; and it is through our relationships with our children that they adopt their values. They will recognize the integrity and security of the moral order and the dependability of righteousness only if we let them experience such in their lives with us.

> The parent—who is gentle with the family pets; who is tender with clumsiness; who shows concern for the scratches and bruises of the youngster; who helps out a sick neighbor—is building an atmosphere in which young people can grow into a healthy tenderness....

The sense of moral values cannot be wedged into a child by admonition. It has to come as the fine flowering of experience.[3]

Paul Tournier has written a fascinating little book called *Secrets*, all of which is very pertinent to this discussion. He points out—indeed it is the thesis of his book—that secrets are essential for the personhood of every individual. "It is to the extent that [a child] has secrets from his parents that he gains an awareness of self; it is to the extent that he becomes free to keep his secrets from them that he gets an awareness of being distinct from them, of having his own individuality, of being a person."[4] Now, this may seem paradoxical, because it is communication and dialogue that we have been talking about and that are so important in person-to-person relationships— and now I'm talking about keeping secrets. But people must become persons before they can really share in a personal way; and herein lies a concept that is very, very important not only to the growth of children but to the development of adults as well.

If you have older children, you realize that there comes a point when that child does not tell you everything, and wise is the mother who can learn not to pry into their secrets. The secret may not be anything grand or really important, but the emotion that a child attaches to it may be extremely important; for that matter, the emotion you attach to certain things make them extremely valuable. "A certain secrecy, to just the right extent, ought to enclose every precious thing, every precious experience, so that it can mature and bear fruit."[5]

A secret is the beginning of a child's assertion of himself. He has something that is unique and all his own. Let him have it. I'm reminded of a rather humorous incident that illustrates the point. There are four little boys at church who are quite good buddies—one of them is mine. However, the four of them are so mischievous that it's almost dangerous to get them all together at one time. But, once one of the mothers had them all over to spend the night and the following day. Of course, all of us were very curious as to what might have gone on. The mother of one was bombarding her son with every question she could think of: What did you have to eat? Where did you sleep? What did you play? Did you behave? and on and on and on. Finally, he'd had enough inquisition and said, "Well, the baby sneezed twice if that's of any interest to you." She deserved that retort.

The mother of one of the high school girls I had in Bible class a year or so ago came to me and laughingly said, "Ann told me that you said in class that girls don't have to tell their mothers everything." I admitted that I had said that very thing. She said, "You didn't need to encourage her; she never tells me anything anyway." I remember that in my own life this was the cause of greatest friction between my mother and me. I'd come in from a date or a party and I wouldn't have my shoes off before she was plying me with questions until I just wanted to scream— and sometimes did. It wasn't that I cared for her to know where I'd been and who was there and what we did. I just wanted to tell it in my own way and in my own good time; sometimes I wanted to think about it for a while before I told anybody. This is still something of a problem between us. I heard her tell someone not very long ago that she'd rather get a letter from my husband than from me because he tells her more of our business than I do. Please do not be irritated with your child no matter his age when you realize he is keeping something to himself; it is absolutely essential for his development as an individual and subsequently as a person.

Some parents become detectives, hiding themselves to spy on their children. One mother of a girl I was much interested in used to take all the scraps of paper out of her wastebasket and put them together to see if she had any secrets written on them. Another listened at the door to hear all her daughter's phone conversations. Others find out in more subtle ways, but their spies are out. With these pressures a child will react in one of two ways: he will become more and more remote, hide more and more from them, live his life completely without their knowledge, close himself from them and perhaps grow to hate them. Or, he will capitulate before them, feel always obligated and guilty, do only the things they say and see only the people they approve. This will lead to illness or to emotional retardation. He will always be immature and dependent.[6] Either situation is cause for serious concern. To intrude upon the private life of your child is to violate his personality and to destroy trust and faith which are the very foundations of the personal relationship that you want so much.

I am not saying that you should never ask a child a question; but there is a great difference in questions and a great difference in motives for questions, and a child can tell whether you are concerned or just nosey. This problem is discussed in a very helpful and interesting article entitled "Ask, Don't Tell." The author had complained to the principal of the high school that her son, though pretending to be listening, seldom heard anything she said. The principal's answer was "Ask, don't tell." She started right in to do just that. The night after the spring dance when her son came in to breakfast, her first question was how the dance was.

"Okay."

"Want to tell me about it?"

". . . Not really."

End of conversation . . .

She kept on trying and she learned lots of things. She learned that "one thoughtful question is worth a dozen inquisitive ones. The prod-and-pry approach makes people clam up." She also learned that "questions must spring from honest inquiry, not from attempts at flattery or efforts to manipulate the other person's thinking."

Sometime later her son came downstairs one evening after he'd been studying and said. "I think Hamlet's an idiot." The mother asked why he thought that. "Because he's putty in his mother's hands." She asked him to explain further and so began one of the most personal dialogues they'd had in a long time. "We started out with Hamlet and ended with a lively discussion of the whole mother—son relationship. It was one of those rare and wonderful interludes when communication flows like wine." The next morning she asked him why he had been so communicative the night before whereas when she had asked him about the dance, he had frozen over. "Well," he said, "you weren't just leading me on. For once I knew you really cared."[7]

The next step beyond the secret is the telling of it. Secrets must be shared as a part of the continuum of growth, and the child must choose the person with whom he shares. Here is the real budding of person-to-person relationships that grow out of the roots of infant love. "By opening out, by telling one's secrets—but freely this time—one becomes personally linked with those to whom he reveals them, and becomes fully a person thereby."[8] When the child has been allowed this freedom, then he can choose even his parents as confidants and friends—and in doing this, affirm them as persons too because they have been chosen freely. And how much sweeter this is— this free interchange that comes from the heart— than the forced and controlled confidences.

The important thing is that you are willing to be chosen, that you are ready to listen, that you care enough to be available, and that you really are concerned about the feelings of your child. About two years ago my son Gailon and I were having one of our difficult periods of non-communication and being completely at odds with each other. I had finished cooking dinner one evening before my husband came home, and I went out in the yard and sat down with the children to wait for him. Gailon came over and sat down beside me and I pushed him over and started tusseling with him in the grass. He began to laugh and then he looked up at me and with one of the sweetest looks I've ever seen on a child's face, he said, "I love you." I was completely disarmed when he did that, not because it's unusual for a child to say that he loves his mother, or even for *him* to say that, but because I suddenly realized how long it had been since I'd given him a chance to say it or even acted as if it mattered. I was ashamed, but I still find myself making the same mistake—not being available and really concerned. Sometimes my other son Jens—who doesn't talk much and whose feelings are hard to read—will say to me after I've heard him pray at night, "Will you stay and let's talk for a little while?" So many times I've said, "Oh, honey, I'm so tired. Let's do it tomorrow" or "I just have too many things to do tonight." I could just bite my tongue out when I've said that.

Your child's memories will be built out of the experiences you share—and so will your own memories. The making of memories is one of the very important aspects of your relationship to your children. No child is too small—not even the tiniest baby—for memories. Oh, he will not recall actually the rocking, the petting, the singing, the laughter; he won't understand the words you say softly to him. "But his disposition will remember. From these things will come a warmth and security, a sense of happiness and love, a deep planted feeling of being wanted and included and honored... which will last all his life and give it meaning."[9]

Memories are easy to make. A walk in the rain, watching a frog family outside the kitchen door as we did several weeks ago, a bowl of popcorn in front of the fire on a rainy afternoon, watching the sunrise, a story read instead of the bathroom cleaned, a day spent alone with Mother or Daddy doing just what the child wants to do, a day of school missed in order to go on a trip with Daddy, making cookies together, shopping for a new pair of shoes. As I think about this, I wonder what memories I'm building for my children. Always busy, busy, busy! If you have several children, you've already learned—I hope—that the work is never done and that the ironing is never caught up; and if I wait until that is done, then the only memories they will have will be of a harassed mother vainly rushing to finish work.

One mother, Mrs. O'Sullivan, said it this way:

> To be friends with your children, to laugh and run and dance with your children is making memories. I hope that when I am very old, one of my children will remind me of the days when I used to dance in the front room with the broom. I hope they will be able to say, "Mother mostly always stopped to read a story," or "My mother was a very funny and laughing mother. Remember the picnics, remember the sea, remember the candy parties and the tea and toast we used to have on a rainy afternoon?"
>
> I shudder to think of my children remembering how clean their house always was. Or how they always had to wear a spanking clean shirt to the grocery store. Wouldn't it be terrible if my children remembered simply that I wouldn't allow them to build a tent in the front room?[10]

The gifts our children need from us are mostly homemade. Attention, affection, praise, laughter, dignity and self-respect. The meaning of discipline and work. Respect for others and a willingness to share. A sense of values, justice, truth and honor. Wonder and enthusiasm. Faith, hope, courage and conviction. The memory of a good home and understanding parents. If all these are wrapped in a love that does not demand or seek reciprocity, then we will know the joy—even in awesome responsibility—of seeing our children become persons and of realizing warm, trusting, sweet life-long relationships with them.

But what about our husbands? Are these same qualities important? Acceptance, concern, sharing, secrets, listening, interest, freedom? Oh, yes!

How many marriages are doomed from the beginning because each enters the relationship with the idea of changing the other or with such an ideal picture of the other that the real person can never be accepted. I know a young girl, recently married, who may be heading for trouble. After just a few months of marriage, her husband was sent to Vietnam. Since he's been away she has thought of a number of ways in which she's going to change him when he returns. Part of what she has said may have been in jest, but sometimes she seems very serious. He'll come home soon. Recently he wrote asking her to take care of a matter for him. She did, but she deliberately did it her way rather than the way he asked. His mother saw what she had done but very wisely didn't say anything. This is the boy this girl pledged her love to just a year ago. Yet, it would seem that she really has not accepted him for what he is.

My husband and I were talking about this recently, and we both agreed that we have changed a great deal in the fourteen years we've been married; but we also agreed that it would have been disastrous (since we both were pretty determined and independent at the beginning) had either of us set out consciously to change the other.

A person who works harder than anyone I know to have a truly happy, Christian home in which each member finds his true fulfillment confessed recently that she had just realized that she has been trying all these years to mold her husband into what she has wanted him to be instead of letting him be himself and loving him for it. She once asked me why he often withdraws, and I think it's because he has to withdraw sometimes into his own little world just to be himself. Perhaps she is more ready now to let him be just "Al."

Two long-time friends divorced after several years of unhappiness and unsuccessful attempts to get along. I've always believed that their basic trouble was that they did not know each other well enough when they married; the extent of their experiences together was playing tennis and engaging in long philosophical discussions. They each had an ideal picture of the other. In the "nitty-gritty" of living she discovered that he was not what she thought he was. She was different from what he believed her to be, and neither was ever able to come to grips with the real "other."

It's possible to alienate a mate even when we are trying to give the very best we have. This often happens, I think, when one is trying to convert the other to his own religious beliefs. Either can be so eager and want so much for the other to have what he or she has that without realizing it, he may be pushing the other further and further away. Keith Miller relates an experience in which he was doing this very thing. He had found something wonderful in his life, a real meaning for which he had been searching intensely for several years. He desperately wanted his wife to share it because he loved her so much. But he was too eager, too determined, too overpowering. Finally one night he realized that he was driving a wedge between them and he said to her, "Honey, I can't deny the tremendous things which have happened to me these past two years because of trying to give my future to the finding of God's will. But I have been wrong in trying to force all this on you. No one forced it on me. I'm sorry I tried...to manipulate you by taking you to all these meetings etc. to get you converted. I am really sorry .... When we got married I didn't sign up to *change* you, just to *love* you ... and I do, just as you are." He then makes an observation of great insight: "How wrong I have been so many times in these past few years in trying to change people instead of loving them."[11]

It is in the inner recesses or soul of marriage that the true nature of the relationship is revealed. Those who build for themselves an inner sanctuary have something beautiful indeed and have experienced what God intended when he planned that two should become one. I am convinced, however, that many marriages have no souls. There are no tender touches; there are no glances of love and intimate understanding. Have you noticed looks exchanged by husbands and wives in public? Sometimes their eyes meet across a room in a crowd and you know they are saying to each other, "I love you very much and I'm so glad that out of all this crowd you are mine." Sometimes a word or incident is mentioned in conversation and in their fleeting exchange you know they have a dear and precious secret; sometimes it's humorous and you can see that they are exercising great self-control to keep from bursting into laughter that no one else would understand. On the other hand, some looks are the most devastating and withering symbols of ashes and bitterness: "You're acting like an idiot and I hate you" or "Just wait until I get you home."

There are the happenings of the day, the thoughts, ideas, dreams and secrets. The degree to which these things are shared is varied indeed, and fortunate is the couple who can freely and lovingly share themselves with each other in more than a physical way. I appreciate the fact that my husband tells me about what happens at work. He has an interesting job and he meets many delightful people, and I like to hear about them. He always tells me the unusual events and often the little day-to-day things. Very often if he has a decision to make he will come home to talk about it before he makes it; I can't make it for him and I never try to do that, but I can be a sounding board for him so that he can more clearly see the alternatives. Too, he listens as I talk of my day and the accomplishments or problems of the children, and he listens to the children too. On the other hand, there are husbands who do not want to talk about work when they get home; they want to forget it and relax and enjoy their families. They're not hiding anything; they just like to leave it behind. The wife whose husband feels this way is wise not to pry but she should also be very sure that she has not dammed the flow of talk by lack of interest. Don't ask your husband what he did at work today unless you are really interested; it would be better to confess honestly that you just aren't really too concerned about what happens on the job.

All of us like to hear tender words of love—and yet there are some men (as there are some women) who simply cannot express what they feel. But they show every day of their lives—by their loyalty, by their faithfulness, by their labor, by their devotion—how much they care and how deeply committed they are. However, Tournier suggests, and I am inclined to agree, that "transparency is the law of marriage and that couples must strive for it untiringly at the cost of confessions" and revelations

about themselves "which are always new and sometimes hard" and that marriage is really a life of
discovering each other. It will come "only by suc-
cessive jerks, by an alternation of withdrawals and
difficult surrenders." Their unity is established
and renewed over and over again by "the exchange
of secrets."[12] No two people will ever know each other
completely; in one sense I guess we're always alone
in the most secret recesses of our beings. But knowing something of the "realness" of the other is necessary for true happiness, for building a wholesome
family atmosphere, for the development of oneself
and the enrichment of the other. Even as we let
the child keep his secret and confide when he will,
so too we must let our partners do the same.

There are areas for some where there can never
be complete understanding and sharing. For example, I have two friends who have exceptional
musical ability and for whom music is a part of the
very fiber of their beings. Their husbands appreciate
this and have provided them with pianos. They listen
to them appreciatively and attend concerts with
them, but they really do not share in the depths of
their souls what music means to their wives. However, this does not erect a barrier between them.
These husbands love their wives enough to let them
cherish and expand their own personalities.

Then, there is the "holy of holies" for people who
are deeply committed to each other: sexual intimacy.
No other physical act is so intimate and has such
potential for real communion. But for many—even
Christians—this beautiful and wondrous gift is only
physical gratification. A friend recently told me that
she had never thought about sex having spiritual

dimensions. For those whose marriages have souls, for those who truly love, for those who have given themselves into the keeping of each other and God, "the communion of bodies becomes the communion of souls. The outward and visible sign has been the consummation of an inward and spiritual grace."[13] Someone has said that "sex intercourse is the great sacrament of life"[14] (sacrament being defined as the physical sign of union with a spiritual reality). Another writer has suggested that "the sexual embrace, worthily understood, can only be compared with music and with prayer."[15] For it to become our "holy of holies" it must be accompanied by constant sharing and continually revealing of ourselves to each other. "When two people love each other, nothing is more imperative and delightful than *giving*; to give always and everything, one's thoughts, one's life, one's body, and all that one has; and to feel the gift and risk everything in order to be able to give more, still more."[16]

To achieve such intimacy takes time, diligence and perception of the moods and needs of each other. Recently, our ladies' Bible class had a party. We have two a year and they are usually "fun" parties. I wanted to go to that one very much, but I noticed that my husband did not seem very enthusiastic. This seemed a bit unusual because he likes parties in the first place and in the second place he will usually go if he knows that I want to go, as I try to do with him if there is someplace he really wants to go. Finally, I asked him if he really didn't want to go. He said, "No, I really don't want to go." I didn't dismiss it immediately because it seemed an unusual response. Then I realized how long it had been since he and I had really visited with each other. So, I fed the children and put them to bed early that night. I fixed steaks for us and we ate in the dining room and had a party by ourselves. We talked about all the things we'd been saving to tell each other. Later, when someone mentioned not seeing him at the party, he replied that we had had just as nice a party as anyone.

I know that there are good marriages—stable marriages, happy marriages—where all that I've mentioned is not realized. There are some instances in which men and women simply cannot express the things they feel in their hearts. There are some where there is no longer the need for much talk; they know what the other feels. There are men who do not understand the temperaments of women. I have a friend whose husband is just as sweet and loving as he can be; he takes care of his family well, provides their needs and many luxuries and is genuinely devoted to them. But he keeps his thoughts to himself. His wife is a deeply sensitive, talented and thoughtful person; but she cannot pour her heart out to him because he simply does not understand what she's talking about. She is a good wife, is very much aware of his needs, and fills them to the very best of her ability. But the fulfillment of some of her deepest personality needs are found elsewhere.

There is so much that might be said about personal relations in the family. To know the joys God intended we must take time: time to talk and confide, time to pray together and worship together, time to sit quietly with each other, time to say loving words, time to engage in loving acts.

Father,
Grant unto us true family love,
That we may belong more entirely to those
   whom Thou hast given us,
Understanding each other, day by day, more
   instinctively,
Forbearing each other, day by day, more
   patiently,
Growing, day by day, more closely into
   oneness with each other.[17]

Chapter Three

The Unspeakable Gift - Christian Community

WHATEVER ELSE THE church has been or ought to be, when it has been a vital, relevant force in the world it has not been a society of perfect or righteous people but a community of loving, caring, compassionate, trusting people. Dr Winfred Garrison in his book, *The Quest and Character of a United Church*, says that one of the major miracles attending the origin of the church was the universal fellowship that was achieved in spite of "racial prejudice, cultural diversity, class distinctions, local pre-occupation, and the difficulties of travel and communication."[1]

Those early Christians were not perfect nor did they always think correctly about their faith; the New Testament testifies amply and in detail to their glaring imperfections. One does not have to read far to be convinced that they were sinful, but they loved each other. Their affection was so characteristic and unusual as to be noted by the outside world. Tertullian, one of the early church writers said, "'Only look,' they say, 'look how they love one another.... Look how they are prepared to die for one another.'" Such community is possible only because of Jesus and through him. Through him the way has been opened to God and to each other.

I believe that we have not properly appreciated the fellowship we know in Christian community. Dietrich Bonhoeffer, the German theologian who spent his last days in a Nazi prison camp and was martyred by his own people, came to understand deeply the blessing of "life together," which became the title of one of his books. He talked about the blessed privilege of living in visible fellowship with other Christians and said, "It is by the grace of God that a congregation is permitted to gather visibly in this world."[2] He called it the "roses and lilies" of the Christian life. How much a momentary meeting with another Christian meant to this man imprisoned and without assurance of another hour of life! He writes of it poignantly:

> The prisoner, the sick person, the Christian in exile sees in the companionship of a fellow Christian a physical sign of the gracious presence of the triune God. Visitor and visited in loneliness recognize in each other the Christ who is present in the body; they receive and meet each other as one meets the Lord, in reverence, humility, and joy. They receive each other's benedictions as the benediction of the Lord Jesus Christ. But if there is so much blessing and joy even in a single encounter of brother with brother, how inexhaustible are the riches that open up for those who by God's will are privileged to live in the daily fellowship of life with other Christians!

> It is true, of course, that what is an unspeakable gift of God for the lonely individual is easily disregarded and trodden under foot by those who have the gift every day. It is easily forgotten that the fellowship of

Christian brethren is a gift of grace, a gift of the Kingdom of God that any day may be taken from us, that
the time that still separates us from utter loneliness
may be brief indeed. Therefore, let him who until now
has had the privilege of living a common Christian life
with other Christians praise God's grace from the bottom of his heart.[3]

There are those who attempt to be Christians
alone; their religion, they say, is between them and
God. Christianity outside of community is a contra-
diction in terms. God in his love and wisdom knew
that "each man needs an experience of life in the
great family of God if he is to grow to understand
the real nature of that love and the real character
of his response to that love, to say nothing of growing
to understand and to live creatively with his fellows."[4] We need the fellowship, the corporateness,
because we are weak and sinful. We need the support
of others who have committed themselves to the pre-
valence of Christ's kingdom on earth. In isolation
we become self-centered and unconcerned. There
is no inner growth, for personhood and Christlike-
ness develop in relationship. Through each other we
find strengthening love and forgiveness, constant
recall to the divine source of our lives, continual renewal of our spiritual citizenship. Belonging, sharing, being accepted give purpose and meaning to
individual lives. "If God ... is truly revealed in the
life of Christ, the most important thing to him is the
creation of centers of loving fellowship, which in
turn infect the world."[5]

Trueblood suggests that it is very strange "in the
light of the Biblical insistence on love as the principal
thing, that we have emphasized it so little in comparison with other elements."[6]

This I command you, love one another (John 15:17)! God himself is teaching you to love one another,... we urge you to have more and more of this love" (1 Thess. 4:9-10, Phillips).

In Christ he chose us before the world was founded, to be dedicated, to be without blemish in his sight, to be full of love..." (Eph. 1:5, NEB).

Live your lives in love—the same sort of love which Christ gives us ... (Eph. 5:1, Phillips).

... making allowances for one another because you love one another. Make it your aim to be at one in the Spirit, and you will inevitably be at peace with one another (Eph. 4:1-2, Phillips).

I can remember from my childhood many sermons on faith and lesser points of doctrine but I recall only one that dealt with love. Often I heard other religious groups criticized because they preached all that love stuff. Usually when we speak of those of religious traditions different from ours, the questions we ask are pertinent to what they believe. Have you ever heard anyone ask how they love? When others speak of us, they mention the peculiarities of our doctrinal content, but I have heard only a very few times anyone comment upon our love and concern for one another. In one place in which my husband and I lived we had an apartment and subsequently recommended other of our friends to the landlady. Never did she turn one down and she said, "I don't know what you preach over at that church, but I do know this—you certainly look after each other and I'm glad to have you as tenants in my apartments." Surely this is the pervasive kind of concern that ought to be more often the mark of our life together.

What has happened to us! We criticize and condemn; we are unforgiving, we are petty and self-seeking. Even in the church we sometimes use others as stepping stones for our own progress. We are thoughtless and uncaring in little ways.

BEARING EACH OTHER

One of the concepts that runs throughout the entire Bible is that of "bearing." I should like to suggest first of all that we have failed to bear one another. One of the Old Testament prophets drew a sharp contrast between the Babylonian gods—the idols—and the God who cared for his people. They have to bear their gods—carry them—but the God of creation and history bears you. In Jesus God bears us as a mother her child, as a shepherd the helpless lamb. He upholds us, he sustains us, he carries us. We are his burdens. We, too, must bear each other, forbear and sustain each other, become burdens borne by love for each other.

I must bear you in your freedom, and you must bear me in my freedom; that is, we must let each other be what we are. "The freedom of the other person includes all that we mean by a person's nature, individuality, endowment. It also includes his weaknesses and oddities, which are such a trial to our patience, everything that produces frictions, conflicts, and collisions among us."[7] More than this, it means to bring ourselves eventually to the place of taking joy in the personhood of the other. All of us have had the experience of disliking a person intensely and then later coming to know the person well, understanding why he acts as he does, and through this process coming to love and appreciate him. There is a lovely person in the congregation

I attend who has been so often misunderstood and misjudged that she has suffered deeply from the barbs. As I came to know her, I knew that I was in the fellowship of one of the most sensitive, most compassionate persons I'd ever known. Another friend did not understand her, had been offended by her, and was somewhat critical of her. When I told her a little bit about the life of the other—the almost overwhelming burdens she carried in her life—the friend said, "I had no idea!" Not long ago I saw these two put their arms around each other and say to each other, "I love you!" They had met person to person. They were ready to bear each other—in love. They are now burdens to each other, but in this lies the beauty of bearing one another. "Walk with all lowliness and meekness, with longsuffering, forbearing one another in love" (Eph. 4:2).

Recently in a class discussion, we were talking about those with personality traits that are irritating or offensive to others: bad tempers, hypercritical attitudes, inability to make decisions, self-pity, incapacity to say "I'm sorry." One of the class members said, "Oh, I don't feel anger or hostility toward them. I feel sorry for people like that because they must be so miserable inside!" These, too, must be carried in love.

Bearing burdens! There are certain needs to which we all rally. If there is sickness or death in a family, we send food to them. If we know of a specific need for clothing, we usually supply that. We emerge with tangible expressions of concern when there are emergencies. A few years ago, a fine Christian family in the congregation of which we were then a part suffered great material damage to their farm from a tornado. Immediately the following day, a number of the men from the congregation went out to help bring order out of the chaos and get the farm in operation again. Where there is calamity most of us respond with generosity and focus our attention upon those specific individuals and families who are affected. This is certainly what we should do; but this is not really what I'm talking about when I discuss "bearing burdens." I'm talking about the heavy loads that people carry in their hearts day after day and year after year—shame, guilt, sorrow, weaknesses, failures. All of us have burdens unique and peculiar to ourselves; some are more pressing and intense than others.

In one congregation of which I was a part one of the members tried to commit suicide. I personally was overwhelmed with shame and remorse because not one of us had taken the time to touch carefully and tenderly the wounds of her heart. We had not cared enough to assure her that she could confidently cry out, "Help me! I need you!" even though we knew that she was living in almost intolerable circumstances. We had not been willing to become involved. We had not helped her feel important and worthy, to make her feel wanted and needed. We had not really let her know that she mattered to us. But we were brought to our knees and to her side by this violent act of despair. As she began to smile and build life again, we were able to show her that our concern was genuine and that we wanted to help bear the burdens.

In our congregation there are many with such problems that are often in my heart and prayers. But I wonder how sensitive we are to their daily needs.

I am not attentive enough. I wonder if we give them the strength they must need through our relationships with them. There are several families who have retarded children. One is away in a school; the mother of another cannot yet bear to give hers up even though it seems advisable for the welfare of the family; one has an adult son who lies senseless and helpless day after day after day. She must keep him in diapers and feed him as a baby, and her prayer is every time she leaves the house that it will not catch on fire. Yet she walks into worship with a smile on her face and the aura of faith about her that makes one know that she has someone who shares the load. The startling thing is that I had been speaking to her for almost three years before I knew of this. There is a widow of a partnership that must have been rare and wonderful indeed! When I see tears in her eyes often, I know how deeply the loneliness is embedded in her heart. She too has a handicapped child. But always a smile—even in tears sometimes—and always an encouraging word for others!

In almost every church there are those who have lost their companions and lived through long, lonely years with only memories of happier days. They do not pity themselves; they lead useful lives. But I wonder how many of them pray as one such woman did, at night in her room, "Oh, God, help me not to show to others the deep hurt I feel." These people do not appear pained as they sit beside us in worship or work with us on various projects, and they are splendid examples of faith for the rest of us; but let's not forget in our hurried lives that there are still scars covering the wounds of sorrow that are easily opened. And let's not deny them friend-ship so essential for their well-being.

There are those whom death has touched recently who need not to be forgotten after the first hours of sorrow are over. There are parents who have suf-fered the pangs of disappointment in children; those with marital failures; those who feel that they have not lived up to their ideals and so are disappoint-ments to themselves and feel that they are to others; those who are rejected by their families, sometimes a husband or wife because of their dedication to the Lord; children whose parents have destroyed them; young people whose temptations are sometimes more than they can bear; those who can face life only with the aid of alcohol or tranquilizers; those who bear the weight of secret sin and guilt that they'd like so much to confess to an understanding friend. The list could go on and on.

But I'm asking this: Do we really help one anoth-er to carry these heavy loads?

A friend of mine, who recently experienced a very tragic sorrow, has written some beautifully sensitive essays about grief—how to face it and how to help others. Here is a part of one particularly relevant paragraph.

I've learned something of the essence of fellowship. In his book *Your Other Vocation* Elton Trueblood makes the point that we must "earn the right" to help, and though he doesn't discuss the point in the context of human suffering, I think it has relevance here. In my own grief those who are helping the most to make it bearable are people who have "earned the right" to absorb some of the sorrow. They are friends with whom I have had warm, personal relationships in the past, who have shared with me their own hopes

and fears and disappointments, who have shown their
loyalty by immovable devotion to me...just as another human being.... The real point I want to stress
is that one of the primary motivations for cultivating
deep, genuine friendships is that these friendships
give us the "right" to be closest when suffering is
greatest. How limited we are without this right! how
blessed with it! We talk a lot about "personal work,"
and I have learned from this experience that those
who do it best are those whose concern is deeply personal. I think we don't really understand the meaning
of Christian fellowship until we know what it means
to be personal.[8]

Have we earned the right to bear burdens—to be
partners in care—by our involvement, by having in-
vested trust in one another, by having taken time
to listen, by letting our hearts be touched, by showing sensitive understanding and care?

I want to insert just a thought here in passing.
If our attitude toward persons is truly unselfish
and loving and out-reaching, then "we must be ready
to allow ourselves to be interrupted by God. God
will be constantly crossing our paths and canceling
our plans by sending us people with claims and petitions. We may pass them by, preoccupied with our
more important tasks, as the priest passed by the
man who had fallen among thieves, perhaps—read-
ing the Bible."[9] It may be that this is the Cross raised
in our path. The work of Jesus was described by these
words: "Surely he hath borne our griefs, and carried
our sorrows...the chastisement of our peace was
upon him." So, it is our fellowship with Jesus and
the cross to experience the burdens of others. Do
we turn away?

I have implied in all this another facet of our mission of bearing: bearing the weaknesses and sins

of each other. "We that are strong ought to bear the infirmities of the weak and not to please ourselves" (Rom. 15:1). Have you ever considered how revolutionary this idea was—and even is to many today? It was the pagan principle that "the weak must bear the burdens of the strong and must not please themselves!"[10] Always there are the weak and to eliminate them would be to destroy the fellowship. Strong and weak need each other, and at some time or another each of us is among the weak. And *always* each of us is weak in comparison to another—if to no other than Jesus. Even Jesus recognized one greater—"the Father is greater than I" (John 14:28). We are so apt to judge and despise and become arrogant with our own pride! Sometimes we even rejoice when another falls. "That the highest strength should be put at the service of the lowliest weakness" is a fundamental teaching of the gospel of Jesus. "Though he was rich, yet for your sakes he became poor that ye through his poverty might become rich" (2 Cor. 8:9). "He who is greatest among you shall be your servant...(Matt. 23:11). And there is that tender scene that is forever etched in our hearts: Jesus—the Master—washing the feet of those stumbling, vacillating disciples—even Peter and Judas. The strong bearing the weak! Jesus bid his life for the miserable, weak, undeserving persons that we are. "If God so loved us, we ought also to love one another" (1 John 4:11). When I stop to think how much I am supported by the strength of others— by those who know my weaknesses and sins and love me still! Where would I be and where would you be if someone had not believed that our weakness could be released into strength? People who cared!

And we can bear only when we know, and we can know only when we are willing to meet person to person.

Even in the church there are young people who are causing a great deal of trouble and who are unusually beset with problems. I don't know how much of what I hear is true, but I do know that I'm tired of hearing adults condemn them and dismiss them in utter disgust. Please don't misunderstand me. I don't in any sense approve of what they are doing, but I think they are crying out desperately for help and for some purpose to their lives. We need to pray for them and their parents; their teachers need to make their relationship to them so vital that they become a moving force in their lives. Someone needs to be real to them and to make Jesus real for them. But we cannot as long as we stand aloof and critical instead of trying to get inside to see life as they see it. How very important it is that the older and more mature surround young Christians with love and understanding!

I would like to inject a thought here that is closely related. It is estimated that churches are losing from 50 to 80 per cent of their young people. The reason most often given is that they go away to college and atheistic professors destroy their faith. For the most part I believe that they didn't have the faith and commitment in the first place. And I believe that one of the reasons is that we have not provided meaningful relationships for them. It is to our shame that far too often the people with whom they seek to identify and whom they try to imitate are not those within the church—not the preacher, not the elders, not their teachers. In my class of high school girls we were discussing teachers who had made a difference in their lives. They all mentioned one teacher they had had that stood out above all the rest. When I asked them the reason, they said, "She cared about us." I strongly believe that the language of relations speaks much more forcibly to a child than the language of words; therefore, we ought to make our Bible classes places where an atmosphere is created in which a child, young person, or adult can grow, express feelings, know what it is to be accepted for just what he is, feel the assurance of belonging, and experience deep, personal love.

Confessing Together

There is yet another facet of relationship that we have neglected. Because we have been so unforgiving and so condemning toward each other and so afraid of ourselves, we have completely ignored the biblical injunction, "Confess your sins to one another" (James 5:16). That's just as specific a statement as "believe and be baptized," but how many times have you ever really done that? Occasionally when we have been wrong we have gone in humility and penitence to the person wronged and admitted our wrong and asked forgiveness. Sometimes we rather laughingly talk about our faults: "Oh, I really do lose my temper too much" or "I guess I wasn't a very good mother today." But we have not developed this grace and blessing of confessing person to person, friend to friend, heart to heart, sinner to sinner.

We find it very difficult to confess because, as I mentioned before, we cannot be honest with ourselves. Somehow we have let ourselves come to believe that the church is a museum for the display of perfect souls, and our pride and self-deception will not allow us to see ourselves as sinners. We dare not admit to being sinners. Bonhoeffer so truthfully suggests that "many Christians are unthinkably horrified when a real sinner is suddenly discovered among the righteous. So we remain alone with our sin, living in lies and hypocrisy."[12] Don't we know that whatever righteousness we have is from God?

Another reason we do not confess is because we do not trust each other. I cannot bring myself to lay open the rawness and bareness of my inner life to you. For all I know, you'll go straight to the phone to call all your friends to tell them the secrets that I entrusted to you. Furthermore, you seem so good that I fear you won't understand or that you may carelessly trample upon the most sensitive recesses of my heart and soul. We want to share with others our goodness, our faith, our devotion and our piety. But we want no fellowship as sinners. Yet concealed sin poisons the soul and separates us from each other. Confessed sin destroys our false pride and humiliates us.

Keith Miller tells about a confession he made in prayer before a friend. Up to that time the very idea had repelled him, but one sin kept hovering in his heart, keeping him in anguish and confusion. When he finally was able to let go, he "realized that once a man has confessed his most awful sins to God *before another person*, he can never again pretend (comfortably) that he is righteous. . . . He can quit wasting so much of his energy explaining himself and making sure that everyone understands that he is a good man. . . . He is a selfish sinner. . . ."[13]

Several years ago I had just about reached the end of the rope with my oldest child. I had three others younger (all within 4½ years) and I guess I was just beaten down. One day I became so incensed with him that I had the urge to hurt him badly or even destroy him, and it was with all the effort I could muster that I quit spanking him when I did. I knew that I had to talk to somebody; but I couldn't. It would destroy the concept of the model mother I thought myself to be —and the perfect mother I had thought I could be before they were born. My self-image would be crushed. But I finally called a friend and said, "I must talk to you!" It was one of the most difficult things I've ever done, but she listened with kindness and love and understanding. She didn't condemn or preach sermons; she knew I wanted to do better. She said, "Yes, I understand, I've felt that way too!" After I had been able to get it out in the open and admit to myself and to someone else that I was not a perfect mother, that these were my feelings and that I needed help, I felt a cleansing, a real desire to get to the root of the problem (which I think was neglect on my part), and a renewed love for my little boy. With complete trust I've confessed to her many, many times since then the burdens of my soul, and she has to me.

Confessed sin loses its power, places us in the path of God's overflowing mercy, enables us to break through to the real fellowship of the cross, to genuine communion with each other, to a new life, and to the renewal of the joy of baptism.[14]

To whom can we confess? To him who lives beneath the cross of Jesus and recognizes his own sinfulness, his own need of confession and the mercy of God. If I confess my sins to you, will you understand—will you still accept me? If you have once been horrified by your own sins and aware that they nailed

Jesus to the cross, you cannot be horrified at mine no matter how rank they may seem to be. You may not understand how in a moment I could hate my child; you may not know how one could be unfaithful to her husband; you may not understand another's weakness for alcohol. But that isn't really necessary. Love and trustworthiness are the essential qualities—the love that "covers a multitude of sins," love that does not diminish the worth of the sinner, and love that respects the secrets of another. Bonhoeffer wrote, "It is not experience of life but experience of the cross that makes one a worthy hearer of confessions. The most experienced psychologist or observer of human nature knows infinitely less of the human heart than the simplest Christian who lives beneath the Cross of Jesus.... Wherever the message concerning the Crucified is a vital, living thing, there brotherly confession will also avail."[15]

We have rejected one of God's sweetest blessings. God has given us each other that we may not be alone in darkness. Being alone with sin is utter isolation.

PRAYING TOGETHER

Praying with another may be a new idea to you, but I can tell you that there's no sweeter moment in a relationship than when you're praying together. It's difficult to do at first; but if you make a beginning, your inhibitions and reluctance will soon vanish (and this is one of the places where confession is easiest—before God and your friend at the same time). I have a friend with whom I pray often; and sometimes when I'm in one of the dark places and can't pray by myself, I can pray with her and feel the nearness of God in her. One day the two of us were together and another friend who lives nearby knew it; she was getting ready to leave on her vacation. She took a few moments from her packing and preparation to come over. She came in, took our hands, and said, "I must pray with you before I leave."

And how often do we hold each other up in prayer before God in definite specific ways. I don't know why it's so hard for us to look at someone and say, "I'll pray for you" or "I know that you're having difficulties and I've been praying for you." Or why is it hard for us to say, "Will you pray for me?" While I was writing this chapter, a friend of mine in another city was trying to cope with several major problems all at once; another friend and I told her that we'd be praying for her at a certain time each day. She said later that she felt such strength in being aware that she was joining her prayers with ours at that particular time. Person to person with God and each other in prayer!

One of the great writers on prayer, Douglas Steere, says that

when we hold up the life of another before God, when we expose it to God's love, when we pray for its release from drowsiness, for the quickening of its inner health, for the power to throw off a destructive habit, for the restoration of its free and vital relationship with its fellows, for its strength to resist a temptation, for its courage to continue against sharp opposition—only then do we sense what it means to share in God's work, in his concern; only then do the walls that separate us from others go down and we sense that we are at bottom all knit together in a great and intimate family. There is no greater intimacy with another than that which is built up through holding him up in prayer.[16]

COMPANIONSHIP

We do not cherish the companionship and share the happiness and joys of each other as we should; that is, we do not participate together in enough meaningful activities. We have lots of parties; life sometimes seems made up of them—class parties, ladies luncheons, receptions, teas. I like parties, but I wonder if we don't often hide in the safety of bigness and overlook the potential for friendship and communion in simpler things. I personally do not like to give big parties. I like small, intimate groups where there can be good conversation, a real sharing of thoughts and ideas, and a person-to-person feeling.

In the rush of today's living we have lost the art of enjoying and sharing the natural and unsophisticated. On one occasion a friend and I took a group of young teenage girls to the beach. We went to a quiet, secluded area and had a delightful time. The girls had taken marshmallows along to roast, and they spent about thirty minutes together gathering wood, digging a hole in the sand, and getting the fire going. As I sat and watched them, I became aware of how much in communion and companionship they were in the simple task. I just never have enough time with my friends and I think I should atrophy if I never saw them except across a bridge table or in large, miscellaneous gatherings. There are so many ways to redeem time and friendship simultaneously. Sometimes, early in the morning, I'll call a friend and ask her to bring her ironing board over; we spend several hours then ironing, talking, sharing ideas, listening to music.

That so many find difficulty in sharing the joy and success of another is mystifying. So often when something nice happens to one within the community—yes, I'm still talking about the fellowship of Christians—the worm of envy begins to tunnel in. We are led to minimize the other's accomplishment, to depreciate the character of the other, to be destructive and juvenile or to feign indifference. Several years ago one of the members of our fellowship was the recipient of a very unusual job opportunity and in connection with it a trip abroad for him and his wife. I couldn't think of anyone nicer for such honor and privilege, but I heard so many snide remarks concerning them.

In one city there is a family who built a beautiful home, one just like they had always wanted. These are among the most devoted and committed Christians I know; they give liberally of money and self and serve others in ways almost no one knows about. But the envy and jealousy and unkind remarks that continued to be evidenced made it impossible for them to enjoy it. They sold the house and moved into a more ordinary one so that the barriers between them and their fellow Christians might be broken down again. To rejoice with another requires maturity and love!

SMALL GROUPS

For the concluding thought of this chapter I want to mention the value of small groups within the church and how they can help us in our attempts to know a genuine fellowship and communion. Now, I don't mean social groups that tend to be exclusive and cliquish and are based on whether or not we play bridge or golf, whether we've had a college education, whether our husbands are professional people or skilled workmen or whether we live in a certain neighborhood or on some other sophisticated criterion.

Many of our congregations are getting so large that many people find it hard to identify and often become lost in the shuffle of numbers. This is particularly true of people who tend to be shy, withdrawn, introverted, and unassertive. I believe that we have overlooked the importance of the small group in helping us to feel a part, to know that we are really seen as persons, to find our place of service and work. There are many ways in which this can be accomplished. Some churches have been divided into zones with leaders who provide guidance in social and spiritual areas and help to make the group a vital one. In other places the Sunday morning Bible classes are the focal point of identification for individual members. Surely, however, the prayer and discussion groups active in so many fellowships are the most effective, for there is more opportunity here for real dialogue and exchange of feelings. I believe that these are the most powerful forces working in many churches. There is a danger in this kind of group that ought to be recognized. It must not become an end in itself, a matter of pride or a retreat from reality. Trueblood points out that "a prayer group which does not make its members more effective apostles in their jobs and homes, and more sensitive participators in the fellowship of those who bear the mark of frustration, is essentially a failure. The test of the vitality of a group does not occur primarily while the group is meeting; it occurs after the meeting is over."[17]

Keith Miller relates in some detail the progress of a prayer and discussion group in which he was involved. He invited several people who were interested in giving their lives more completely to God and in finding out how they might get to know him personally as he is revealed in Jesus. They divided their evenings together into three sections: first they shared the problems and discoveries of the week, secondly they studied the Bible, and then they prayed together. Many things happened during their year of sharing together; he tells of their struggles to be honest and to be real witnesses outside the group. It was not their immediate enjoyment that was important but discovering that living Christianity is very different from what they thought it to be. "We found that it is actually...*real* creative life, life in which we are free to be honest about ourselves and to accept and love each other and Him, because the Living Christ is in the midst of us.... Suddenly we had something real to tell, something 'which we have seen and heard'!"[18]

Bearing each other, our burdens and our weaknesses, confessing our sins, sharing our happiness and achievements, praying together in small, accepting, loving groups: these are person-to-person activities that will enable us to become the company of loving, caring, compassionate, trusting people that Christ surely intended his church to be.

Our Father, be with us as we work each day with others, and keep us ever mindful of thy teachings of love in our relationships with others.

Help us to understand each other. Help us to understand ourselves.

Keep us from forcing our opinions on others. Guide us so that we do not create a climate of threat and defensiveness around us, but instead one of freedom in which we ourselves and others can grow as Christians.

Let us never forget that we cannot make people be committed Christians, but that by the practice of love we can help others become committed. And let us always remember that as we practice love and understanding we ourselves become witnessing Christians. Amen.[19]

Chapter Four

Beyond The Circle

THE STORY OF THE Samaritan and the "poor old beat-up man" (as my little girl says) is one of the most frequently studied in all the Bible. We've all known it from childhood. Yet, I think we have talked all around its real meaning. It is rather painful to face what Jesus was really telling the lawyer who asked him such a simple question: Who is my neighbor?

What does Jesus really say in this story to this arrogant Jewish man of the law, who felt exclusive, proud of his heritage, assured of his status among God's specially chosen people? He knew what the law was, and he had the code for his life wrapped and tied in a little confining box. He knew who his neighbor was—his fellow Jew and no one else; but Jesus smashed his cosy little world with what must have had the same power and effect as a hydrogen bomb. Jesus looked into his eyes and asked a stinging question: Which one of these men proved to be "a neighbor?" Don't you know his sense of loyalty to his religious leaders was pounding in his breast? Don't you know it must have almost choked him to have to admit that it was this loathesome, despised Samaritan? But he had to say in all honesty that it was the man who had showed mercy. Then Jesus looked at him again and I imagine in a quiet but commanding voice said, "Go thou and do likewise."

I don't know what this man's life was subsequently, but I imagine that he was often haunted by the thought of that traveler on the Jericho road! His constricted "world of doing good to those whom he knows and likes is suddenly enormously and painfully extended to all those who need his compassion and help. Jesus will not allow true religion to exist in comfortable little circles of its own. The new quality of life is love in action, and that may mean coping at firsthand with the difficult, the messy, and the unpleasant. Again and again Jesus teaches that love must go beyond the limits of ordinary human niceness and kindness.... 'Your love must be like the perfect love of the Father, who is kind to the unthankful and to the evil....'"[1] No matter how ugly the wounds, they must be touched. Jesus identified himself with humanity—not with its perfect specimens—but with the blind, the deaf, the dumb, the mentally deficient, the repulsively sick, the beggar, the outcast, the lonely and friendless, the racially and socially unacceptable. His friends were strange: fish merchants, greedy tax collectors, a one-time prostitute, a high society woman.

In a way, this is the most difficult chapter for me because I know that I'm going to say things that I'm sure some of you will disagree with and suggest some ideas that are a bit ugly to contemplate. I ask only that you search your own hearts in the light of Jesus' life and teachings.

BEYOND CLASS

Jesus taught us that we must go beyond our self-sufficient cliques of relative wealth, decency and middle-class morality. Everyone stands in need of compassion—thief, drunkard, woman of beauty, man of wealth, child without care, Negro, prostitute, the man ground to dust in poverty. Everyone needs Jesus. Please let me etch this upon your hearts. Do you remember the time when Jesus was eating in a certain house with many "bad characters" (as one translation puts it)? The righteous Pharisees rather sneeringly asked his disciples, "Why is it that your master eats with tax-gatherers and sinners?" Jesus heard them and said, "It is not the healthy that need a doctor, but the sick. Go and learn what this text means, 'I require mercy, not sacrifice.' I did not come to invite virtuous people, but sinners" (Matt. 9:10-13). We, however, are prone to invite the virtuous and hope that the sinners will stay away. There are worlds all around us that we know nothing about and we sit with consciences untouched by man's inhumanity to man. We do not feel the tragedy of all things that live in the presence of impending death.

Elton Trueblood in *The Company of the Committed* points out that one of the most dramatic analogies by which Jesus points up the mission of his church is that of *penetration*. Think of all the metaphors he used that have this basic idea in them: the *salt* of the earth, *the light of* the world, the true *bread* from heaven, the living *water*, *leaven*. There are many others and the effect of all of them together is clear indeed: "The Church is never true to itself when it is living *for* itself.... Its main responsibility is always outside its own walls in the redemption of common life."[2] And I'm saying to you and to myself that this must be done in a personal way, for love is personal. I'd like to mention to you some of these worlds where we have failed to take love and warmth and understanding, where we have failed to offer person-to-person relationships.

We have not gone beyond our decent circles to the prisoner and the person of disrepute. He's dirty and sinful and we do not want to contaminate ourselves. I have read the story of a Presbyterian church group in Vermont that began to realize their mission of penetration and try to be the church "out there." This was one of the results: A group composed of young couples was studying the servant passages in Isaiah, where God was telling Judah that her mission was to be that of the suffering servant to mankind. Jesus later uniquely took this mission upon himself because his people had failed to discharge it. He became the suffering servant. These young couples decided that this role was the one they must adopt if they were to follow Jesus. They began to make weekly visits to the county jail. On Sundays they reported back to the congregation. Some of the inmates had never before been really seen as persons, but the class members took time to hear how "it" happened. When important, they visited families of prisoners or their former employers in order to effect reconciliation if possible. One man who had stolen an automobile and raped the daughter of a leading citizen expressed fear of the town's anger toward him. He felt that he'd be all right though if he could just walk down Main Street once. On the day that he was set free one of the class members walked down Main Street by his side.[3]

I'd like to contrast that example with the attitude in a congregation of which I was a member several years ago. Through the influence of one of the members who was a very competent and dedicated man the opportunity came to help in a rehabilitation program for some men about to be released from the state prison. It was discussed in the business meeting and this was the response: "No, we want nothing to do with it. What if they should come to church here? What about our children?" What would be your response? What would be Jesus' response?

In a well-known church in one of the congested, melting-pot metropolitan areas of our country, the minister said of the work of his assistant minister: "We don't need the riff-raff and niggers that are coming out of his counseling program." God help us if this is our attitude. We erect barricades to keep people out, but it was to the "riff-raff" that Jesus went. He did not (as we do) classify individuals by their families, their clothes, their schools, their degrees, the part of town they live in or the amount of money they have. "There were not people who were his type and those who were not. He invited them all to be his friends."[4] He looked into their hearts and eyes as persons. They knew when he looked that they were somebody; he knew when he looked they had the power to become more than they were. It was a person-to-person relationship.

There is a lovely, elderly lady who lives in Tennessee whom I have known since I was a young girl. There are men scattered the length and breadth of this country who call her "Mother." They will proudly say that she was the greatest influence in their lives, that had it not been for her they would be nothing. For about fifteen years she taught in the Tennessee State Training School for boys (there were both young boys and older men). On the first day of class she found bitter, resentful eyes bearing down upon her. She walked unsteadily across the room and wrote one word on the board—L O V E. They could not read it and she did not tell them what it was. She began to talk to them about what a wonderful word it was, how understanding *it* could change their lives, and how understanding other words could further change their lives. At that moment she began to teach them the fundamentals of an education; but more significantly, she began to love them, to trust them, to treat them as persons, to develop person-to-person relationships with them. She allowed them to keep her car within the compound and to keep the keys. They kept it shined as bright as a mirror and always in proper repair; and when she wanted it, she'd send for one of them to bring it around to her. She was warned that one day they'd bolt with her car and she'd never see them or it again. She didn't believe it. Often she'd take a group of them to town or for a ride on Sunday afternoon. Her friends predicted that they'd kill her, take her money and car, and escape. She never gave it a thought. Many of the boys and men served their time, went off to war, sent her their money to keep, wrote "Dear Mother," came back, married, and now bring their children to see her.

She tells of one runny-nosed, dirty, unkempt little fellow who came and cried his heart out for a week because he had been separated from his little sister. Nothing about him was attractive, but her heart went out to him and she tried to find his little sister. She found out that the child's father had tricked him into a misdemeanor so that he'd be caught and taken to the school so he (the father) wouldn't have the responsibility of his care anymore. This little boy grew to manhood, married, has a lovely family, one of whom is now in college. Through the years he has gone back to see the only "mother" he really knew. He has never forgotten the lovely teacher who loved him and turned his weakness into strength.

This man recently wrote in a personal letter to me:

> My mother died when I was 6 years old, shortly after I was sent to the State Training School. This is when I first met Mother Peebles. I was lonesome and home-sick but she was always there kind and interested. She took my mother's place for me. She would get herself in trouble protecting us boys from the cruelness of the guards. When we were beaten she would not make us sit in her classroom. It was against school rules to let a boy stand after a beating. She protected many a boy from getting a beating, she felt this was never a just punishment.... She often told me she would like to take me home to live with her but it was impossible, she was supporting her own family. It still made me feel good to know someone wanted and loved me.

He left the school and, when he was old enough, went into the service. "All the time I was in service she wrote to me and sent me packages. While in the service I had an ... operation and Mother Peebles took the trip to La. just to visit me. She was the only one I had...."

He told me about his family and then this: "We also have two little foster boys living with us.... We feel Mother Peebles' influence had much to do with our decision to take them. Her being so kind to me when I was small made me realize how important it is to a small child to feel wanted and loved."

There were others of her boys who did not do well. They progressed to major crimes, and many times I've seen her on her way to jail with cigarettes, cookies, and magazines. Once one of her former students was accused of a rather heinous crime; as soon as she knew it, she went down to see about him. The jailer did not want her to see the boy. "What do you want to see that boy for? He's not worth seeing. I hope they hang him. He's nothing but scum!" She looked at him with her kind but piercing eyes and said, softly, "He's human and he needs love and compassion just the same as you do. He means something to me and I'd like to see him." The jailer dropped his head and led her to him.

How many boys and men, considered the scum and riff-raff of the earth Mae Peebles loved and believed into new life! We need to go where Jesus went. In these lonely outcast souls we must see Jesus.

BEYOND RACE

We have not torn down the barriers of race and color. Looking briefly at the church's activities is cause enough for shame. The church has not been a leader in breaking down walls of prejudice. Church-related colleges were the last to admit students of all races, and some church-related orphanages and homes for the aged are still segregated. A number of our white churches have even gained national prominence for refusing to allow Negroes to worship with them. One of our fellow Christians—a Negro—at the end of a searching article made a heart-rending statement: "The burden of being a Negro in this nation is not an easy cross to carry, and I regret to say that my experiences in the church have not made it any easier."[5]

Jesus did not establish two churches, one for whites and one for blacks. Can you imagine Jesus having a church, a group of people that physically have taken the place of his body on earth, in which people can not sit down together at the same table to eat or sit down in the same pew to worship? God forgive us for the travesty we have made of the cross!

A Negro minister, speaking several months ago to a group of preachers and church leaders who were mostly white, looked into their eyes and said, "How can you men master philosophy, Greek, theology and not accept my humanity-ness?" He told about how as a boy the white preachers would come to preach at his little congregation and wouldn't even shake hands with his Negro brethren. They'd put their hands in their pockets or they'd use them to hand out tracts. Then he looked at them almost pathetically and cried out, "I want you to feel as frustrated as I am."

Only as our hearts change individually can the church change. I believe that one of the reasons we cannot meet those of other races, and especially the Negro race, is that we think they're different, that their emotional and physical makeup is not like ours, and that they are blanketly inferior. I'd like to share an experience with you that had a great impact upon me.

In one of the small towns where my husband often filled the pulpit on Sundays there was a faithful Negro family. We sensed very soon that they were not really accepted as a part of that church community, even though people spoke to them, shook hands with them and sat beside them. One Sunday the mother asked my husband if he would come by to talk with her about some things that were troubling her. She couldn't quite bring herself to openly say what was on her heart to a white man, but the picture was not blurred. She felt lonely, isolated, unaccepted by the white Christians. She hinted that the preachers and their families never came to their house for dinner as to the homes of others. My husband assured her that we ate wherever we were invited and all that she had to do was to put her name on the list (the accepted custom there since all the preachers who spoke for them drove considerable distances). I guess she didn't have the courage to actually write her name there beside the names of all the white people but she invited us for a certain Sunday and we went. When we were asked by another member of the congregation where we were going that day and told him, we received the quietest, stoniest stare I've ever felt in my life. We had a lovely afternoon with this warm, genuine, thoughtful family. I became very much aware that day of their "human-ness." The blackness has nothing to do with that.

They had a record player with a collection of music that they liked to listen to just as we do. They had photograph albums preserving their sweetest memories just as we do. On their walls and shelves were the mementoes of their lives. There was a young grandson, and for a very wonderful hour or two he played the piano and sang and sometimes we all sang together. Music bound us, as it often transcends all barriers.

In this home was a lovely daughter who had a sweet, cultured voice; and her mother had worked hard that she might have voice lessons. I couldn't help wonder what opportunities she would ever have to use this; could she find acceptance and would her mother be able to see her child realize her dreams? I might add too that she was one of the most poised, gracious young girls that I've seen. Her mother sent her in to talk with us while the finishing touches were being put on dinner and she handled that assignment with a rare graciousness in one so young.

There was a little nephew in the house that day— the age of one of my children—and he was picked up and loved and kissed just as my own were. I recalled the revealing incident in *Huckleberry Finn* when Huck and nigger Jim had run away. One morning Jim told Huck about how he had treated his little girl. She had had scarlet fever but had recovered. One day Jim told her to shut the door. She just stood there. Several times he told her and she just stood. He went over and slapped her and sent her sprawling. When he came back she was standing in the door with tears streaming down her face. He started after her angrier than ever, but just then the wind blew it shut and the child still didn't move. He said his breath almost came out of him and he went over behind the child and yelled. She didn't budge. "Oh, Huck, I bust out acrying en grab her up in my arms, en say.... De Lord God Almighty forgive po' ole Jim, kaze he never gwyne to forgive hisself as long's he live! Oh, she was plumb deef en dumb, Huck...en I'd ben atreat'n her so!" Huck realized something he'd never known before: "He was thinking about his wife and children, away up yonder, and he was low and homesick; because he hadn't ever been away from home before in his life; and I do believe he cared just as much for his people as white folks does for their'n. It don't seem natural, but I reckon it's so . . ."

One of the most haunting books I've read in a long time is *Black Like Me* by John Griffin. John Griffin had his skin darkened by a medical process and lived for several weeks as a Negro in the deep South. One reviewer called it "a stinging indictment of thoughtless, needless inhumanity. No one can read it without suffering." The humiliation he suffered for no reason other than the color of his skin was incredible, and the "hate stare" that he felt over and over again was unreal! Toward the end of the time when his skin was getting lighter, he would change back and forth from the role of Negro to white; there was all the difference conceivable in the way he was treated and in the privileges he enjoyed from one day to the next as his skin was darker or lighter. But in one poignant instant we see the "innermost being" of the Negro heart and soul.

It was night and he had been walking and hitchhiking all day with very little to eat. As he continued on his way, eating what little a white couple would sell him from their highway store, a car stopped to pick him up. It was a Negro man, and Griffin told him his problem—tired—dead-tired—and no place to sleep. The man said he had six children and only two rooms but that he was welcome to go with him if he didn't mind sleeping on the floor. They drove down into the forest, up a rutted path and soon came to a shanty of unpainted wood, patched at the bottom with a rusting Dr. Pepper sign. His wife stood in the door waiting for him. The children laughed and shouted welcome. They thought it must be a party because there was company and this was unusual indeed. There was only a pot of beans for supper but they were willing to share, and Griffin added his loaf of bread to the meal. Later he sliced his Milky Way bars into thin slices for dessert and the children ate almost rabidly a delicacy they'd never known before.

He congratulated the man on his lovely family and the mother spoke of how blessed they were to have healthy children. The "father's tired face" became "animated with pride." "He looked at the children the way another looks at some rare painting or treasured gem."[6] The children asked Mr. Griffin about his children. Did his children go to school and how old were they? He was acutely reminded that it was his daughter's birthday, and they were excited to know that she'd have a party with candy just as they had had a few moments before.

> But it was time to go to bed, time to stop asking questions. The magic remained for them, almost unbearable to me—the magic of children thrilled to know my daughter had a party.... The children kissed their parents and then wanted to kiss Mr. Griffin. I sat down on a straight-back kitchen chair and held out my arms. One by one they came smelling of soap and childhood. One by one they put their arms around my neck and touched their lips to mine.[7]

They all lay down on their thinly-padded pallets and Mr. Griffin went to his, but he couldn't sleep as he lay there fighting mosquitoes which made the children jerk in their sleep and thinking of his daughter's birthday party. He got up and went outside in the cold. "I thought of my daughter, Susie, and of her fifth birthday today, the candles, the cake and party dress; and of my sons in their best suits. They slept now in clean beds in a warm house while their father, a bald-headed old Negro, sat in the swamps and wept, holding it in so he would not awaken the Negro children.

> I felt again the Negro children's lips soft against mine, so like the feel of my own children's good-night kisses. I saw again their large eyes, guileless, not yet aware that doors into wonderlands of security, opportunity and hope were closed to them.
> It was thrown in my face. I saw it not as a white man and not as a Negro, but as a human parent. Their children resembled mine in all ways except the superficial one of skin color, as indeed they resembled all children of all humans. Yet this accident, this least important of all qualities, the skin pigment, marked them for inferior status. It became fully terrifying when I realized that if my skin were permanently black, they would unhesitatingly consign my own children to this bean future.[8]

Don't you know that that Negro mother's heart beats for her child the same as the white mother's does for her child? Don't you know their kisses are just as sweet? Don't you know she wants her son to be able to grow up into useful manhood, to be able to get an education, to be able to find employment commensurate with his abilities, to be loved and to be accepted socially for the person he is? Have you wondered how they feel when they see their children tormented and mistreated? They feel the same as any other human; they know what love is unless they have experienced only hate and rejection as many of them have, they pray to the same God, they feel hurt and heartaches just as any other. They have needs for affection, for friendship, for achievement the same as you and I.

We often wish that we could make a dramatic witness for the Lord, and it seems that there aren't really many ways to do it in our civilized country. We'd like to do something in which the difference which Christianity makes is piercingly clear, but we are hard pressed to know what such an act would be. The persecution of our missionaries serves in some vicarious kind of way to satisfy our desires to suffer for the Lord. Trueblood suggests that "one of the few areas in which a courageous witness is possible today is that of racial brotherhood."[9] In New Orleans in 1960 there were only two parents out of two thousand who had the courage to walk past a jeering and obscene mob to take a little girl to school. Since that time many have fearlessly aligned themselves with the cause of humanity and justice. Some have even lost their lives because of their dedicated involvement in efforts to restore personhood to those who have been robbed of it in the complexities of our society. Most of us will not be called upon for such bold activity—and I am not suggesting that any of us must grab a banner and march. But day by day— in little ways—we are going to be called upon to change our attitudes, to open our hearts, to show God's mercy, to be Christians in an un-Christian world.

I have a friend who not long ago was given the opportunity to make a wonderful witness for Jesus in her life. By virtue of her husband's position, she was active in the women's auxiliary of his organization. I believe that she was to be the president of the group for the year. But a problem was facing her.

There were now Negro employees whose wives had to be asked to come. The meetings were usually held in the homes of various members and already some had stated decisively that their homes would not be open to the Negro women nor would they attend the meetings where they were present. Her question to me was, "What shall I do?" I couldn't tell her what she should do, but I hoped she sensed that the Lord had opened a door for her and that through his grace she could walk through it.

I don't know how rigid the walls of prejudice and hate are built in your mind, but I know that we will die spiritually unless we can let the love of God flood through our hearts, unless we are willing to witness personally in this area. I believe with all my heart that race problems will never be solved until we are willing to look behind the fact of color and see the image of God, until we are willing to say, "Come into my living room, eat at my table, be my friend, and let's share our feelings and longings!" Heart to heart!

BEYOND COMPLACENCY

We have not penetrated the ghettos of poverty, destitution, and nothingness. Oh, we've given cans of food, cast-off clothes, Christmas baskets, welfare money; and we've kept them "in their places." The bureaucracy of agencies and government has made objects and numbers of these people and manipulated them so that they are no longer persons; they are ground into non-personality; they are dreamless and hopeless. In the church I feel that we have so often done the same thing. We have not given a genuine compassion and love; we have given dutifully out of our abundance. Perhaps we have given stones instead of bread.

I heard the writer Jan de Hartog say that it is not poverty itself that defeats a man but rather the dehumanizing quality of the help he receives and the personal rejection he sustains. The poet Vachel Lindsay said this too as he contemplated the world's wrongs:

> Let not young souls be smothered out before
> They do quaint deeds and fully flaunt their pride.
> It is the world's one crime its babes grow dull,
> Its poor are ox-like, limp and leaden-eyed.
>
> Not that they starve, but starve so dreamlessly,
> Not that they sow, but that they seldom reap,
> Not that they serve, but have no gods to serve,
> Not that they die, but that they die like sheep.[10]

In our pockets of destitution young souls *are* smothered out, the poor *are* ox-like, limp and leaden-eyed. A crust of bread and a worn-out pair of shoes will not remedy this. In fact, a week's supply of groceries and new shoes will not remedy this. There must be those who care enough to give them hope by becoming involved in personal relationships and who see their importance as persons.

We often complain because the person we help seems not to respond or to show gratitude. The Overstreets point out in their book, *The Mind Goes Forth*, that it is impossible for this kind of man to feel grateful because in his deprivation, whether emotional or physical, he is angry with you because your life looks so easy and you seem so removed from his. In the second place, he is not given what he really needs.

What he needs is a basic sense of security and self-respect. Nothing that anyone can give him *from the outside* can, for long, satisfy his inner lack. He can pretend gratitude, and even feel a brief semblance of it. But when his inner problem resumes command over him—when his deep insecurity and anger at life surge back—he will translate his lack of satisfaction into a feeling that he has not been given enough: that he has not been given what is properly due him. The sense of having been given a raw deal . . . by virtually everyone and by life itself, is simply not compatible with gratitude for receiving.[11]

I have a friend, Laura Peebles, who is one of the very few people I know who truly does without things in order to do for others. Ever since I've known her (since she sensed the need of a very young girl for a caring older friend) she has had some person or some family or sometimes several in whom she has a genuine interest and with whom she has a genuine relationship—those who need the help she can offer. She doesn't just give old clothes and food to them; she tries to help them find some meaning to their lives. Four or five years ago she was talking with me about the family she was interested in at that time. She was discouraged; they didn't seem to respond to her overtures. There was an older girl about whom she was particularly concerned; she wanted to see her take some interest in herself as a person, to act more refined, perhaps, to learn good manners. I said to her, "Laura, if that is all she's known for sixteen years, she isn't going to change so easily and in such a short time. Be patient with her." Recently I talked to her again about the same family. She said, "You know, they never said 'thank you' back in those days because they just didn't know to do that." She has been able to help the father keep jobs to do, and he now takes pride in helping people keep their yards looking pretty, whereas before he did only what he needed to do to get by. She had wanted to give him a lot to put a little house on since his family was just shifted about from place to place, but he wouldn't let her. He saved the money himself to do it. It's a poor lot, rocky and hilly, in an out-of-the-way place. But it's his, and he bought it himself. Five years ago he had no idea this could ever be possible and he didn't really much care. But now he has some self-respect and feeling of responsibility for his family.

Ministering to people like this is difficult, but they need redemption and love too. A few churches have seen this great need and responded to it. Several of the churches in Houston have established a little mission in one of the lower social and economic areas of our inner city. Among other activities there are classes throughout the week. It is the hope of those participating to teach these children and adults about God and his love. But how can they, when some of them have never had an experience of love? One lady was making the rounds to pick up some of the children one day, and she found a little girl sitting all huddled up outside in a corner with her face to a wall. She tried to talk to her but the little thing would only shrug her shoulders. The only words she uttered were "The door's locked." What will happen to children like this unless they have some kind of caring, warm personal relationship? Will we sit them down at tables and drill them on the facts of the birth of Jesus, or will we pick them up in our arms—dirt, sores, bad smells and all—and love them? Really love them! *Touch the wounds*!

These areas, of course, also become pockets of crime and delinquency, but there is an answer even to this. In the book, *A Parent's Guide to the Emotional Needs of Children*, there is a lovely story about how profound influence can be. A sociology professor sent a team of research students into the slum area of a large city to find the potential delinquents. He had worked out certain criteria by which they could be spotted. Twenty years later he sent the second research team to find out what had happened to the children "spotted" by the first team. How surprised they were to discover that these children had not become delinquent at all. They had turned out quite all right both morally and socially. As they began to seek for the answer to this turn of events, they heard the name of a certain teacher mentioned everywhere they went. Well, they needed to find out about her. They discovered a gentle, white-haired old lady in a home for retired school teachers and questioned her.

"Those boys? Yes, I remember them well. I loved every one of them."[12] Someone has suggested that the most hardened delinquent could be saved if we could give him love enough to match his need.

Jesus said that he had been anointed to preach to the poor. I often wonder where he would walk day by day if he were in Houston or Denver or Chicago or wherever you live. I'm not so sure that it is where *I* transact the business of living.

We have shunned those with loathesome diseases, deformed bodies and disturbed minds. Francis of Assisi, who was known for his embracing of absolute poverty and for his tender care of the sick and poor and lepers, confessed that he would ride out of his way to avoid a leper because he could not abide the smell. One day when a leper sprang into the road to beg alms, Francis spurred his horse to get away as quickly as possible from the sickening sight. Suddenly realizing that he was keeping a room closed to God, he returned, jumped down to embrace the leper and gave him all that was in his purse.

I doubt that we'll ever have to face a leper, and yet we may face a cured leper. It is possible now to cure leprosy, and if it is caught in time this can be done before there is disfigurement of the body. Yet, those who have been cured or in whom the development has been arrested often find themselves unwelcome with former friends and rejected by employers. The crippling symptoms of a promising and popular young athlete were diagnosed as leprosy. The progress was rapid; but as his condition was becoming desperate, the sulfone drugs that can cure this dreadful disease were discovered. However, the damage had been done. He was so crippled and misshapen that wherever he went people stared and moved away, his old friends were ill at ease; even his parents moved to another town. Finally, a kind man gave him a job in a small office, but he avoided people. He'd wander along at night in the empty streets or on the beaches. Finally, it was too much when some Halloween pranksters called out, "Look at him.... He doesn't need a mask." In desperation he sought out Bishop Sheen, whose work with lepers he had read about. The bishop let him spend himself in sobbing out his story and then he set out to help him bear his burden. He did not preach to him; he became his friend. In his busy, busy life he found time to invite Scott to eat dinner with him about once a week. He helped him find and furnish a small apartment. When he appeared on television, he'd invite Scott to sit in the audience. He told him honestly, "You will never have many friends...but those you do have will be true friends." As Scott began to realize that he *was* cured and to be grateful for that, to appreciate those at Carville, the leper colony, who were working so unselfishly, and to comprehend the gift of friendship that the bishop had offered, he began to find his way out of despair. Gradually, others have come to see him as a person because he can now see himself as one—and he did gain new friends. "He feels alive again. He realizes that his life will never be completely normal, but he has found the strength to meet the problems he faces. Friendships now seem precious as rubies. The simplest act of companionship—a date for lunch, an afternoon at the beach with a friend, an hour of conversation—these are moments to be cherished."[13] I wonder how many people we allow to drown in loneliness and despair who would cherish just an hour.

For a number of years until her own recent illness prevented it, Beth Welch of Houston, Texas, was a familiar figure, moving graciously and lovingly through the wings of a hospital whose very name is a dreaded one, for most of its patients are terminal cases.

It began when she was persuaded by a friend in ladies' Bible class to go "hospital visiting." In about an hour they had covered three major hospitals; when they stepped out into the fresh air from the corridors of this one after a few hasty smiles and pats the friend heaved a sigh of relief. "I'm always so glad to get out of there," she said. "It's so creepy and morbid to know they're all dying. I don't know what to say to them."

Beth's heart was touched with the great need for dedication to the task of reaching out in love, even to the dying and to their families. She went back to that hospital and it was the beginning of a rare ministry to people. She found those who were away from home, who had no one with whom to talk and who knew they were dying. She often sat long hours with them letting them pour out their hearts, writing letters for them, playing games with them. When their families came, she helped them in any way she could. One patient led on to another. She still receives letters from wives, mothers, husbands: "You were so kind to him—how could I have made it if you hadn't been there."

Beth became a stagehand in the unfolding drama of life and suffering and death. She saw anguished families; lonely, dying souls; neglected ones hungering for love and reassurance; persons diminished to nothing but pairs of sad, fearful eyes and tubes—but persons yet who wanted a smile and the sound of a gentle voice and who tried to smile amid the tubes. She saw the sadness and beauty of death. She learned to laugh with those who laugh, weep with those who weep, share silence with those who wanted to be quiet, pray with those who wanted to pray. And in her self-forgetful way she truly suffered with those who were suffering, for often when she clasped a hand clinging in physical agony, her body too was in pain. Surely Beth Welch was the channel of God's love, and light and comfort in the shadowy halls of death. She learned the secret of person-to-person relationships with those whom most of us like to avoid. She went not where her own needs could be fulfilled but where there were affection-hungry, lonely, fearful people, many of whom were not at all pleasant to look at, many of whom were bitter and hopeless. Jesus, too, often went to these people. Do you remember when he reached out and touched that leprous man—a breach of social and medical law, a loathsome thing? We don't have to do anything so drastic perhaps, but we do need to open our hearts and eyes to those who need a message and touch of love.

Once Jesus said, "When you give a lunch or dinner party, do not invite your friends, your brothers or other relations, or your rich neighbors; they will only ask you back again and so you will be repaid. But when you give a party, ask the poor, the crippled, the lame, the blind; and so find happiness. For they have no means of repaying you; but you will be repaid on the day when good men rise from the dead" (Luke 14:12-14, Phillips). Have you ever done this? What do you think would happen if you did?

"Wherever the gospel has gone, its characteristic fruitage has been service for all sorts of men in the faith that all sorts of men are worth serving."[14] Of the master it was said that "he had compassion on them" (Matt. 9:36). Compassion, surely, is the Christian virtue, for everyone stands in need of compassion—and compassion seeks nothing in return. Orthodoxy in faith and belief, worship, prayer, are absolutely worthless and become a mockery if they do not lead us "beyond the circle of [our] little group of Christian friends and across the barriers between social, racial and economic strata to find the wholeness, the real closeness of Christ, in that involve-

ment with the lives of His lost and groping children
whoever and wherever they may be."[15] Beyond the
circle!

Compassion is the Christian virtue,

More than righteousness,
Or humility,
Or truth-seeking,
Or patience,
Or zeal,
Or even faith
And hope.

For everyone stands in need of compassion,

Thief,
Drunkard,
Woman of beauty,
Man of means,
Child without care,
Animal,
Bird,

And compassion seeks nothing in return.

To feel
The tragedy
Of all things
That live
In the presence
Of impending Death
Is compassion.[16]

Chapter Five

The Alabaster Jar

MANY FRIENDSHIPS HAVE been immortalized in literature and history. Tennyson's poem "In Memoriam" was inspired by the death of his deeply loved friend Arthur Hallam. His sorrow was intensified as he saw the "dark house...where my heart was used to beat so quickly, waiting for a hand." There were times when he longed "for the touch of a vanished hand, and the sound of a voice that is still." The friendship of David and Jonathan is one of the classics of all time. Its description is surely the formula for genuine friendship: "the soul of Jonathan was knit to the soul of David, and Jonathan loved him as his own soul" (1 Sam. 18:1). Between the older woman Naomi and the younger woman Ruth there was a very rare and tender bond. In Ruth's pledge to her mother-in-law there is epitomized the loyalty, the care and the responsibility of true relationship.

There are varying levels of friendship and different purposes served in various relationships. However, there are a few in each person's life who stand above the rest, a few who are intimate "soul" companions. These are the ones who reach into the very recesses of our beings, who share our inner lives and with whom we share the quest for the things of the spirit and the meanings of life. In them we repose explicit trust, to them we confide our dreams and most exalted feelings, from them we receive confidences and secrets, and for them we feel unremitting concern. Too, it is with these friends that tears flow freely without embarrassment or need for explanation. Their hearts are retreats where we can withdraw to puzzle out our problems, to cry out our sorrows, to live through our weaknesses, and to be more truly ourselves than with any other. We can show our worst selves if need be, assured that this friend knows that underneath there is something better and more real.

One morning during the time I was working on this chapter, just after I had pushed the children out the door for school, one of my very dearest friends came in. When I looked at her I knew something was wrong, and I suppose she knew the same when she looked at me. We were in a sorry state that morning. Both of us were upset with our husbands—it was pretty bad for it to happen to both of us at the same time. Our husbands had waltzed out to work, not realizing at all they had done anything to upset us or to destroy the beauty of the day. We mentally packed our bags but had nowhere to go, so we took our husbands apart and said all the nasty, ugly things we were thinking. We felt sorry for ourselves and sympathized with each other and then we prayed for help with our feelings, for a spirit of understanding and forgiveness and for our husbands. I couldn't have had this experience with just anyone, but with her I could vent my darkest feelings because I know that she knows that I love my husband and am very grateful for his love and patience. I know, too, that she and her husband have something very lovely and lasting, and I know how deep her love is for him. We both knew unquestioningly that we could trust the other. These were momentary emotions, but we needed to get rid of them so that they wouldn't be harbored in our hearts and poison our relationships. If another had come to my door that morning, I probably would have acted as if nothing were wrong. With a true and trusted friend I could be completely sincere. "Oh, the comfort the inexpressible comfort, of feeling safe with a person, having neither to weigh thoughts or measure words, but to pour them all out, just as they are, chaff and grain together, knowing that a faithful hand will take and sift them, keep what is worth keeping, and then, with the breath of kindness, blow the rest away."

We must be very careful, however, that we don't kill our friendships because we never have anything but the negatives to share. There are those who would stifle us and bear us down with nothing but troubles, thinking that in this the intimacy of friendship is born. But this is not true. Not until the friendship has matured and we have earned the right to share the secrets of each other is there real meaning in this.

What can you share with a friend? A song. A stroll along the beach looking for shells. A rose that has just bloomed. A book you have just found. A new insight into the meaning of life or God. An evening walk. An excursion with all the children. An anecdote of the day. A concert. A record. A look. A smile. A handclasp. But more than this we share the deepest longings and yearnings of our hearts. Our dreams and ambitions. The ideas that would seem silly and meaningless to others. The shame that we feel because our lives do not reveal our ideals. The desires to surrender ourselves more completely to God. We communicate from the very core and center of our existence.

Essentially, what does one person give to another? Eric Fromm in *The Art of Loving* suggests:

> He gives of himself, of the most precious he has, he gives of his life. This does not necessarily mean that he sacrifices his life for the other—but that he gives him of that which is alive in him: he gives him of his joy, of his interest, of his understanding, of his knowledge, of his humor, of his sadness—of all expressions and manifestations of that which is alive in him. In thus giving of his life, he enriches the other person, he enhances the other's sense of aliveness by enhancing his own sense of aliveness. He does not give in order to receive; giving is in itself exquisite joy.[1]

Emerson has pointed out in his classic essay on friendship that "our friendships hurry to short or poor conclusions, because we have made them a texture of wind and dreams, instead of the tough fiber of the human heart." They are often surface and superficial because we do not share from life's center.

The special friend is the kind of person we just want to be with. It doesn't matter whether or not we talk or whether we do anything at all. If someone should ask us what we did or what we had to eat we might not even remember. The important thing is that we were together and we found the inspiration and the stimulation for a moment of renewal in life. It is the friend whose arrival can cause us to tremble, the one with whom we can pick up where we left off even though we have been separated for months.

It is this friend with whom we can be silent and in the silence find life recharged and find the soul of each other. These are the hours when we move beyond communication to communion: when we are very conscious of the presence and personality of the other, when we are very sensitive to the ideas, ideals, the spiritual quality, the very uniqueness of the other and are very susceptible to everything the friend is and are aware of what he thinks and feels. We are present to each other and interested in nothing other than gaining the inspiration, insight, peace and joy which come through this mutual communion.

Douglas Steere suggests that "nearly all the great experiences of loyalty, of love, of suffering take place beyond the spoken word." He relates the story of the old Indian who "spoke of how he loved to feel where words come from." This is a lovely thought: "to feel where words come from." He goes on to say this: "Only when you can walk or ride or paddle a canoe or sit by the fire with a companion and be in most active fellowship with him without the need for conversation do you really know and trust each other.... There is a gathering of warmth, a revelation of the inner nature of each, and a charging of the positive bond of friendship if the silence is a living one in which you enjoy each other...."[2]

At the time of a growing and deepening friendship, I sat with a friend one evening as the tears streamed down her face. She was in the depths of a great struggle with her soul. "What's wrong with me—why can't I find the way?" she sobbed. I had no answers for her because she had to find her own. But we sat quietly for a long time with no words being spoken at all. Occasionally I'd reach out and take her hand to let her know that I cared and that I was suffering too, that I loved her and knew the darkness of the shadows. Then, after a while, she said, "I've never before been able to be quiet with anybody." Since that time, there have been many pregnant hours of quietness and communion between us. Something happens to your life in these times — something quite indefinable and indescribable—but just as surely known and felt as if it were tangible to the touch. It is here that profound influences on your life are felt.

In this kind of friendship there must be a mutuality, a fulfilling of the needs of each other, a willingness and ability to be loved as well as to love, an openness to receive and accept. The inability to receive openly and graciously is perhaps one of the greatest hindrances to human relationships, one of the barriers that keep us from meeting person to person. There simply cannot be this kind of deeply loving, outgoing, fulfilling friendship unless you can allow yourself to be loved.

One of my college roommates was a Chinese girl. The girls in the dormitory tried to be kind to her, but it was hard, for she rejected our kindness. One night soon after she moved in with me, she was without sheets for her bed because she had washed her only set and they were not yet dry. I went to a drawer, pulled out my extra set and tossed them over to her. It was no calculated move on my part: I would have loaned them to anyone in the dorm. In fact, my previous roommate and I had kept our linens together and just used whatever we needed. However, my new roommate was offended by my offer, refused to use them, and slept on the bare mattress that night. Well, you can imagine what that did to me. Life went on this way for several weeks and perhaps months. Finally, one of our older and wiser friends took her aside for a talk and explained to her that in rejecting all overtures from those who wanted to be her friends and who wanted her for a friend, she was stopping the flow of goodness from heart to heart. Only then was she able to begin to be able to give herself and to receive graciously and gratefully.

Often when we are recipients of help, encouragement, gifts, or favors, the wheels of our minds begin to churn feverishly, as we try to think of some way to repay. Genuine love does not keep account books; true concern is above arithmetic. Repayment may insult friendship. Do you remember when the woman rushed from the crowd and impulsively broke upon Jesus an alabaster jar of costly ointment? In a moment of overwhelming affection and gratitude she did "what she could" and in doing so was lifted beyond herself into transcendent devotion. It was a dramatic moment and could have been an awkward situation. But the heart of Jesus was touched. He was moved, and with understanding appreciation and warmth he made one of his most compassionate statements: "she has done a beautiful thing to me." If we could only learn to respond with such graciousness and gentleness when someone breaks the perfume of his heart upon us.

Fosdick points out that "no suffering on earth is more tragic than great love hindered in its desire to bestow."[3] A former counselor at San Quenten suggests that among the prisoners a factor as important to their situations as not being loved is that they have no one to love. He observed how pitiable it was when a dog found its way into the compound and was almost killed by the men rushing upon it to pet it and love it.

I think, too, that in such friendships each must be aware of the fulfillment of his needs by the other and that in what he gives to the other is life. A friend of mine who recently lost the close friend with whom she had lived for six years wrote a letter to other friends. It reveals two significant thoughts: her deep appreciation and understanding for the other and the realization of the needs that her friend supplied.

As I view her life sentimentally, I think that the quality I most depended on was her almost infallible judgment and perception. When Dixie made an evaluation of people or situations, she was right—in this respect like Tennyson's friend Hallam whose arrow always hit the eye of the target.... I depended on her perception when I needed her to clarify and interpret my thoughts to others, and such times were frequent. Where my words were often a facade, hers always erected the complete structure—architecturally perfect. Losing this part of Dixie hurts the most, for there is no replacement. But, too, her wit which was both fresh and sharp; her appreciation of each person's uniqueness and her stimulation to us all to be our best selves; her integrity which I never saw her sacrifice for her personal aims; and her spontaneity which never approached irresponsibility—these traits, along with her judgment and perception, contributed a security to me that I feel will be permanent.

I think that here lies the key to being able to receive—in admitting and being honest about our needs, in realizing that we need other people and in maturing to the understanding that real living

is interdependent and not independent. This does
demand some of our pride because in one sense it
is humiliating, but I think there can be no genuine
love without genuine humiliation.

Many of you, I am sure, have read Gladys Taber's
monthly column called "Butternut Wisdom." Often
she mentions in memory her friend Jill who died
several years ago. Theirs was a rare and unusual
friendship. Both of them lost their husbands quite
early in life when there were still children to be rear-
ed. They joined forces to make a home together and
through thirty years their lives had been intertwin-
ed in the deepest companionship—educating their
children with their pooled resources, seeing them
married, and finally having the grandchildren come
now. Jill died and immediately upon reaching home
from the hospital, Mrs. Taber was reminded of the
great emptiness in her life and of the needs so lovingly satisfied by Jill.

> One of her lists still lay on the kitchen counter, writ-
> ten in her firm, slanting hand as steady and even as
> her temperament.
>
> There wasn't, I noted as I went past, a single thing
> on it that lay within my capabilities, not even mend-
> ing the garden gate and shoring up the kennel fence.
> Call Ed Koch was the last item. This meant that she
> *knew* the washing machine was out of order again,
> although I hadn't mentioned it. Jill always did the
> telephoning, since I am afraid of telephones. My clas-
> sic failure was when the barn burned down and Jill
> was saving the dogs and called to me, "Get the fire
> department."
>
> I got the fire department all right, after getting
> the Waterbury hospital, the Apothecaries Hall, and
> an irate strange woman. Or rather, the long-distance
> operator in Waterbury got the Southbury operator

to get them. For some reason this went through my head as I picked up the list.[4]*

Her children came that night and rallied around her in help and efficiency. She was reminded that on any other occasion she would have wanted to share this with Jill.

> Jill and I would have sat up late talking about how wonderful our children were. It was our habit to sit up far into the night and discuss and evaluate the day's happenings. . . .
>
> But, of course she was not there. I had so much to tell her. I wouldn't, now, have anyone to tell all the silly things, the important things, or just the things. For years I had lived in the world of her understanding. I would, I thought, have to stop being myself and be a reasonable, rational woman and not so emotional. With her death, my real self had to die and that was all there was to it.[5]

Responsibility, respect and care are essential elements of the kind of relationship of which I speak. Without these, friendships can degenerate into possessiveness and exploitation. There are immature and insecure individuals who want to have complete power over others and to transform them into things or personal possessions. Too often we seek only to appropriate the personalities of others to ourselves. This is a travesty on love. True friends bring out the best of each other. We want those we truly love to grow and unfold for their own sakes and in their own ways, not for the purpose of serving us or as mere objects for our use. We want our friends to become the best they are capable of becoming; we want their talents and abilities to shine and expand. We must give them room to be themselves and to

*From ANOTHER PATH by Gladys Taber. Copyright © 1963. by Gladys Taber. Published by J. B. Lippincott Company.

help provide the atmosphere in which they can realize their potential for growth and life.

Another condition to guard against is exclusiveness. Love, basically, is an orientation to life, overflowing in concrete expressions. I cannot really love you without loving others. Otherwise the attachment is indrawn and self-centered. There is no jealousy. Each true friendship should enable us to reach out more and more to enfold others and to embrace all of life.

Jesus knew the sacredness of earthly friendships. He, too, knew the inner longing for those who cared, who understood, who were willing to share his moments of darkness and trial as well as the triumphs. Among his disciples there were three who had a closer affinity to his soul than all the rest. He took them with him to the mountain to share one of his most celestial moments. Note that they wanted to stay. Here I think is another of the lessons of friendship. There will be moments of exhilaration and transfiguration with friends, but we cannot stay on peaks that are saturated with such intensity; we must also share the straight, level, and often monotonous paths, the commonplace hours. These three went with him to the Garden—but he left them and went alone a little farther. There will be times when there is a way we must go alone, and no matter how dear the friend, he cannot go with us. But may we always be able to "watch and pray"! Peter, James and John could not. They slept through the ordeal of his soul. How it must have stung when he said, "So, could you not watch with me one hour?" Yes, there will be times when we must watch and pray when there is no other possible way to help.

Then there were Mary, Martha and Lazarus whose home was a favorite retreat for Jesus. There is not a more beautiful picture of the person-to-person relationship than that of Mary sitting at the feet of Jesus, both, I am very sure, pouring out the burdens and joys of their hearts to each other. I shall never forget a Bible lesson that I heard about a year ago when my husband and I were visiting friends in another city. An elderly man was teaching the class, and from his face radiated such warmth and love and genuine emotion; it was evident from every word, from every gesture, from the very tone of his voice that he was in love with life and in love with people. The lesson for the day was about Jesus and his Bethany friends. He said, "Do you know why I think he liked to go there so much? I think he wanted a little petting. He wanted to feel an arm around his shoulder and hear someone say 'I love you.'" I thought to myself, yes, I expect that is exactly right—a touch, a smile and a listening heart.

Such friendship as I've been describing is a garden that needs cultivation; it is based on choice but not on rejection. Though it is true that love is far-reaching and all-embracing, we choose our friends. Who can explain what draws persons to each other? Friends are necessary for a full life. The desire for friendship is the desire for fusion with other souls, for finding the way out of the loneliness of life. But it takes time, just as all else that is worthwhile. I find, however, that it isn't the amount of time as much as it is the nature of the experience in whatever time we have—and there is so much more time if we plan well. I have mentioned ironing together—taking care of a chore but using the time for friendship as well. You can get so much talking and sharing done in two or three hours of ironing. Sometimes a friend and I will study together. We're quiet and not saying much, but we're together. Mending and sewing can be done with another—oh, so many ways to use time. But there must be a constant vigilance. Emerson warns that "it should never fall into something usual and settled, but should be alert and inventive." Love does not take for granted though it trusts and knows assurance. Authentic friendship never grows tiresome; we look forward to eternity when it will continue to flower and blossom and bear fruit. Always there will be the feeling that Mrs. Taber had: "We had so many things to do."

The kind of relationship and love of which I have been speaking are, I believe, gifts from God. Yet, we accept them so casually. So seldom do we ever think of how much our friends mean to us, how much a part of us they are and how much life is enriched because of them. It's a moving thing to contemplate how others love us in spite of what we are, believe in us, and, yes, even enjoy us. How often have you thanked God for your friends? How often do you let them know that you cherish them?

Jesus' prayer for his disciples in the seventeenth chapter of John is a lovely expression of his gratitude. All through the prayer he keeps talking about "those whom thou hast given me." There is unmistakable pride in them—"I am glorified in them." Do you feel yourself glorified in your friends? Surely it was the supreme compliment that he had made known to them all that the Father had given him—the opening of his heart to them and to us.

I love you
Not only for what you are,
But for what I am
When I am with you.

I love you,
Not only for what
You have made of yourself,
But for what
You are making of me.

I love you
For the part of me
That you bring out;
I love you
For putting your hand
Into my heaped-up heart
And passing over
All the foolish, weak things
That you can't help
Dimly seeing there,
And for drawing out
Into the light
All the beautiful belongings
That no one else had looked
Quite far enough to find.

I love you because you
Are helping me to make
Of the lumber of my life
Not a tavern
But a temple;
Out of the works
Of my every day
Not a reproach
But a song . . .[6]

Chapter Six

Friendship With God

I HAVE COME MORE and more to the conclusion that it's almost impossible for a person to have a real relationship with God until he has known a loving, fulfilling relationship with another person. How can a child who has not known a father's love or a substitute for it possibly understand the concept of God as a loving Father? How can a person feel and sense a spiritual love when he has no feeling for and from another human being? I believe that the burden of loving placed upon us is perhaps far more crucial in God's plan of redemption than we have realized. In the October, 1966, issue of *Christian Woman* there was a very gripping article written by a man who had grown up in the squalor and dirt and bitterness and neglect of a slum. It was entitled "No One Cared"—"not even the pigeons cared for the dirty little boy who sat on the curbstone with nothing to do except build up a towering hatred for the shabby world." At sixteen hatred, violence and death were his constant companions. Even in the Navy he was a misfit and an outcast. As he wrote, he was preparing to move soon to a mission work. Contemplating past and future, he said, "My only purpose now is to wear myself out in his service" and "to proclaim that someone cares." But between the bitter, sinful, fearful, unloved slum child and this beautiful relationship with God was someone who loved him and who could show him what it is to love and to trust and to forgive—the girl who became his wife, who led him to Jesus, and who would be by his side as he went on this new venture with God.

Love is complex, many-colored, many-splendored; but the most beautiful aspect of this life-giving quality is the uniqueness of each love relationship. Everyone loves differently. Your gift of love is not like anybody else's gift. That which is between each one of you and your mate or your children is not the same as the love I know with my husband and my children. The relationship with each friend is different and shines in its own beauty and light and adds its own luster to the heart. Each friend sheds a different light to play upon our own; each one calls out something different from us, each one sees in us different possibilities. Friendships are as vari-colored as snowflakes are varishaped. No matter how small, how insignificant you may think your love, if it is genuine and sincere, it is a gift no other can bring. Let me go a step further and say that this love of which I am talking is not a personal achievement. It is a gift of God himself. We can never of ourselves come to this loveliest of attributes. "God's love has been poured into our hearts through the Holy Spirit which has been given to us" (Rom 5:5). We don't fully understand this love, and we won't until we stand with him face to face; but he has given us assurance of its reality.

This is an overwhelming thought: God is person and personality can exist only in relation to other personality. We are the very outpouring of his person. Oh the compliment he paid us by the gift of something of himself! And when we are most like what he created us to be, then we are most like him. We find God walking in the Garden with Adam and Eve; we find him there even after they had sinned and broken the relationship. The idea is that here was a close, intimate relationship, a companionship, a friendship that God sustained with the crowning glory of his creation.

It is even greater astonishment that God needs us. To be sure, he does not need us in the way that we need him, helpless and hopeless as we are; but his love cannot be poured out unless there is a response in us.

Buber speaks to this thought in a beautiful way:

> You know always in your heart that you need God more than everything; but do you not know too that God needs you—in the fulness of his eternity needs you? How would man be, how would you be, if God did not need him, did not need you? You need God in order to be—and God needs you, for the very meaning of your life.... There is divine meaning in the life of the world, of man, of human persons, of you and me.[1]

The great men of faith in the Bible are those who knew the meaning of this companionship. God came to Jacob in the most unlikely of places and told him, "Behold, I am with you and will keep you wherever you go" (Gen. 28:15a). You remember others: Abraham "the friend of God," Enoch who "walked with God," and Moses, "whom the Lord knew face to face." And there were those magnificent prophets who walked on the mountaintops with God calling his people back to him: Isaiah whom God cleansed with a coal of fire, Jeremiah crying out to God in the anguish of his soul, Hosea seeing the people forsake God as his wife had forsaken him. God said, through them, "My people are destroyed for lack of knowledge." He wasn't talking about the knowledge of facts or of the law, for they knew these. The word "know" as it was used over and over again by the prophets is the same word used to describe the sexual relationship of husband and wife. These people had withdrawn themselves from God and man. He might have said, "My people are destroyed for lack of relationship."

But we must be very careful not to usurp a position that is not ours. We are not equal to God. He is God, Creator, Father, Lord and the idea of chumminess with God is cheap and superficial. Our relation to God must be approached with reverence, respect and awe. There is something, I think frivolous, over-sentimentalized, and unfitting about such songs as "My God and I." There is no depth here. An adventure with God is more than flitting through easy and pleasant days as with a golden fairy, going through flowery meadows, laughing, jesting. Don't misunderstand: I think God is in our laughter and our happiness; but walking with God is a challenge in its most profound meaning. There will be suffering and storms. He will not take away these —he never promised that he would—but he will walk with us. And there is the beauty, the peace, the comradeship. His presence with us will be stronger than our troubles, temptations and problems although it is true that he will make even more luminous the sunny times. It seems to me that some of the current attempts to make God contemporary come very close to profaning the majesty and dignity with which

God should be approached—as, for example, the man who began his prayer, "Dear Heavenly Daddy" or the woman who said, "God is a living doll—a real nice guy" or those who currently refer to him as the "Big Cat." When Jesus used the name "Father," it was never jaunty or familiar. It had "the hush of reverence" and "something deep and still."[2]

There are many inroads into the person of God. Just to be with another and sense God through a Christian friend is a rare blessing, and I think that this is one of the reasons he gave us each other. Whatever of genuine love and compassion and kindness there is in any of us is from God and is of his nature. I was talking with someone some time ago whose father had died recently. This was a deeply moving and sorrowful experience for her, for she and her father had a very unusual friendship. I don't remember the exact context of our conversation, but in the course of it she said, "But I get confused. I don't think I know how to distinguish between Daddy's love and God's love." I said, "Oh, I don't think there's any difference. Whatever is real and true in your Daddy's love is God." She said, "I never thought of that." I thought that idea was all mine, until after I had written this the first time I found this statement in Walter Russell Bowie's *The Master*: "That which is most beautiful in men *is* God. The purity, the courage, the love, and the devotion which shine in the great souls are partial lights of the one light of God. And if any man express the perfection of human possibilities, then in and by that fact . . . he is the incarnation of the life of God."[3]

I do not believe that one can come to a knowledge and understanding of God through nature or through aesthetic experiences, but I do believe that in these places myriads of people have felt a spirit and have sensed a presence beyond themselves. For those who know God these times are unquestionably times of communion and fellowship with the Creator. For those who are faithless or unaware they are reminders of something beyond self.

> Some who think they have never had a religious experience have really had one through beauty without knowing it. If you have ever felt your spirit lifted and enlarged in the presence of a great canyon or waterfall, or a majestic storm, or a flaming sunset, or the soft hush of summer twilight, or the play of northern lights, or the flashing of stars in illimitable distances—then you ought not to say carelessly that you have never had a religious experience. If you have ever sensed something holy in a baby's smile or an old man's face, in an early morning bird-song or a great oratorio, in Beethoven's "Hymn to Joy" or in a forest of pines ... then the presumption is strong that you have grasped something of the meaning of worship. ... Worship occurs when you feel yourself in the presence of that Power upon which you and the universe depend. When you perceive, however dimly, that you and this Power are *together* and you feel yourself both small and great before this presence, then you are worshipping.[4]

The two ways in which we most completely enter the heart of God are through Jesus and through prayer made possible by Jesus. It is, of course, through the Word and through his Spirit in our hearts that we come heart to heart with Jesus; but I believe that our great weakness is that we have come away with only words instead of a friendship with our Lord. To know another it is essential to be with him, to have time for acquaintance to grow. How much have you been with Jesus? When we read other books—novels, especially—or see a movie or a play, we experience life with the characters. In our imaginations we are with them or we are the persons they portray; there is a vicarious experience, an empathy. But we read the Bible with such dull eyes —no creative vision, no imaginative insight—fact after fact, precept upon precept. Whenever I've studied the life of Jesus in a Bible class, we've had little question books that pile detail upon detail and smother one with boredom. No wonder our young people see nothing to emulate in his life. The great figures of history are presented to them in greater glory than the Lord Jesus Christ is.

Have you walked with him through the uneven streets of his village home, past the flat-roofed houses and the women drawing water and gossiping at the village well, past the doorways where they sat weaving or kneading dough, laughed with him as he chatted with the children playing funeral or wedding or mother and daddy and children—and then climbed up the hillside slopes where the men tended the vineyards, stopping here and there to talk and listen? Have you wandered through the carpenter shop with him, watching him make a plough or carefully shaping the beams for a new house? Have you climbed with him to the top of the nearby hills and looked out over the broad vistas of fertile land and seen the sun dip into the Mediterranean and watched the sails of the Roman ships bringing legionnaires to the coastal cities? Have you been for a holiday with him—picnic lunch in leather pouch— over to the Sea of Galilee to sit and meditate upon its banks and talk to the fishermen as they brought in their catches and cleaned their nets on the shore?[5]

Have you felt the crowds press against him and felt strength in touching him? Have you heard the gentle, yet commanding, voice say the words of healing, and compassion and love and authority as perhaps he called out a demon or called one forth from the dead?

"Take heart, my son, your sins are forgiven."
"Cheer up my daughter, your faith has made you well."
"Lord, if you will, you can make me clean.... I will; be clean."

Have you felt his eyes gaze tenderly and beseechingly into yours and call:

"Follow me and I will teach you to catch men."
"Come to me, all of you who are weary and overburdened, and I will give you rest...for I am gentle and humble in heart and you will find rest for your souls."

Did you see tears flow down his cheeks as he looked out over the spiritual wasteland of Jerusalem and with outstretched hands cry out:

"Oh, Jerusalem, Jerusalem, killing the prophets and stoning those who are sent to you! How often would I have gathered your children together as a hen gathers her brood under her wings, and you would not."

Have you sat with him on the hillside or beside the sea and listened to his words of life, the beautiful lessons on love and God's Kingdom?

"The kingdom of heaven is like a treasure...."
"The kingdom of God is within you."
"Unless one is born anew, he cannot see the kingdom of God."
"God so loved the world...."

Have you felt his eyes burn into yours and heard him say as he said to Peter, "You can be more than you are." It must have been almost funny when he told Peter he was a rock. At that time Peter was anything but a rock—more like shifting sand: vascillating, fearful, cowardly, impetuous. Eventually the transforming power of Jesus made him just that. And that young John—the son of Thunder— prompted by his mother to look for a prominent place in the kingdom, who later (or so the apocryphal stories go) with his white hair flowing about him would visit the churches who always wanted a word from this one who had been with the Lord: "Little children, love one another." And if we walk with the Master as they did up the valleys of transfiguration and into the Gethsemanes—he will make us more than we ever dreamed even in our finest hours. But we must walk with him as more than a casual bystander, an objective observer, a newspaper reporter. We cannot truly claim friendship until we have felt his heart pulsing with love for all of humanity—and for each. We must sense as we walk with him his constant consciousness of God.

As you sit with him on those Galilean hillsides you must know that it is not only the sweep of land that lies before him but also the sweep of history— the history of his people, of God's chosen people, the history of their life with God. This was the battleground where the blood of his fathers had mingled with pagan blood. These people had believed that a Reality had spoken to them with an authentic voice. They worshipped a living God and however deep the breach between their worship and their lives, a Hebrew boy could not grow up without a sense

of God. Surely Mary's son was even more sensitive
as he brooded over the meaning of these events and
over the real intent of the Scriptures that he had
been taught in the synagogue. Even in his boyhood
and young manhood—the hidden years—he had unquestionably lived deeply in the spirit, else how could
he have moved so easily to teaching men the things
of the spirit? "He who was to show to the poorest
human creatures the glory of God had first found
for himself the glory of God through the ways of
human seeking . . .⁶"

There is no question that his disciples knew that
something of "measureless significance" had happened to their Master at his baptism and during
his stay in the wilderness immediately following it.

It must have been one of their most intimate moments when he shared these soul-stirring events
with them. I wonder if you have stood there beside
the Jordan and watched him covered in baptism and
realized that it was not his own salvation he was
thinking of. He was demonstrating the epitome of
"self-forgetfulness by which the great soul identi-
fies its spiritual fortunes, and its very life, with
the life of others." It was here that he was beginning his role of the suffering servant and associa-
ting "his own soul with the burdens and needs of all
his brethren"—with mine and yours. It was here that
the purposes of his life were beginning to unfold.⁷

Have you agonized with him in his temptation,
or have you just read it as a story? These were not
merely personal trials in a time of weakness. He was
struggling with the alternatives of his life in ways
beyond those in which we'll ever be tempted. What

did his special relationship to God mean? His son-
ship?

Have you spent all night with him in prayer as he
went back over and over again to the source of his
power? Have you seen his countenance change in
prayer as did the three with him on the mountain?

Have you stood before the cross and seen the agony and suffering, the utter loneliness? We cannot
hang there with him, but we can see the anguish
in his face and in the tautness of the veins of the
body—not just physical pain—oh, much more than
that: the mental and emotional agony of sin and
guilt that he bore for us.

It was the good news of the Kingdom of God on
earth that he preached. What men could not do,
God could. As he was about to leave them, Jesus
talked to the disciples about the Father:

> "If you had known me, you would have known my
> Father also (John 14:7).
>
> "He who has seen me has seen the Father (John
> 14:9).
>
> "... the Father is greater than I (John 14:26).

Primarily, Jesus made possible a new relationship with God, the relationship that had been broken
back in the Garden of Eden. He had pled, guided,
invited and punished, but everything he had offered had been abused. But he loved us still and sent
Jesus to show us the way. Jesus was God seeking
for us. G. Campbell Morgan says it beautifully:
"Out of the infinite spaces there comes to me a great
love song. Out of the bosom of the Father comes a
message of tenderness and compassion."[8]

Have you heard the love song? He made it possible for us to be friends with God again. Through

baptism we identify with him as he did with us and come back into companionship; and then he made prayer possible as the way of communion and repeated surrender.

Prayer at its peak, prayer refined and disciplined, prayer of real communion is the finest and most elevated experience within reach of the human soul. Such prayer, however, does not come easily, no more easily than the life of deep friendship with another human. Fosdick aptly suggests that "praying [is] a lesson to be learned by assiduous practice.... We would not expect to take a try at a violin once in a while and yet make much of it. But see how we treat this finer instrument of prayer!"[9] Still further he emphasizes the necessity of perseverance and practice: "How clearly then must the sense of God's reality be a progressive and often laborious achievement of the spirit! It is not a matter to be taken for granted, as though any one could saunter into God's presence at any time, in any mood, with any sort of life behind him, and at once perceive God there."[10] If we approach prayer life with such attention and purpose, the thought of God is transformed perceptibly from mere belief to devotion and friendship. Prayer then becomes a living relationship with God. His life begins to pulse within our own so that we more and more can give ourselves to his purposes for us.

The beginning point of prayer—of vital dialogue with God—is a natural and willing and overwhelming response to the outpouring love and concern with which God confronted us in Christ Jesus. It begins with accepting gratefully the grace and redemption God offers. If the relationship is genuine, then our responses and requests are authentic. Or perhaps they become more authentic in proportion to the depth of our gratitude and the extent of our ability to yield and put ourselves at his disposal so that he can do in and through us what he wants. Within the framework of such fellowship our petitions flow without selfishness or anxiety and with complete trust that it is in him that life knows fulfillment and not in the things we request.

How do we bring ourselves into this intimacy with God, into a confident sense of his presence? The characteristics of this relationship are the same as we've talked about in the preceding chapters. First of all, there must be a mutual reaching out to each other. God is there first, always waiting for us in openness and love; but he waits for us. He will not force himself upon us. Always with him as with others there will be alternate giving and withdrawal, keeping our secrets and divulging our secrets. Yes, God waits for us to tell him our secrets. He does not take them as his own personal inroad into our lives until we give them to him freely. He respects us as persons enough to wait just as we wait for our children, our husbands, our friends to divulge their secrets.[11]

God has told us secrets. He has chosen us as confidants. He speaks to us as conversational partners. We are free to listen or to ignore, to answer now, years later or not at all. "Revelation is the communication of God's secrets by God himself. We would never know anything for sure about him, his mercy, his intention, his work, his plan, if he had not said it himself. . . . He speaks to each of us; he is personally interested in every one of us; he speaks personally

to each of us and he listens to each of us personally."[12]

In our talking with God more than with anyone
else there must be an honesty and transparency.
The thought that you may not be honest with God
may upset you, but so much of the time we're not.
If we're really honest, we may have to dethrone some
of the most egotistical images of ourselves and give
up our selfish goals. Is it not fear of self-awareness
that causes us to resist all but superficial praying?
Being in God's presence will change us. "I dare not
stay as I am and come near to such a love as his."[13]
There is great pain in turning loose of that which
holds us back. Fosdick points out that evidence of
our dishonesty lies in the discrepancy between our
prayers and what the most dominant pursuits of our
lives are evidenced to be.

Keith Miller tells of his experience in trying to
be honest in prayer:

> I realized that my closest relationships had always
> been with those who knew the most about me, and
> loved me anyway. So I began to reveal my inner life
> to Him, all of it. . . .
>
> In trying to be totally honest I found a new free-
> dom and sense of being accepted. For now I didn't need
> to gloss over my true greed and lust and excuse it as
> being insignificant. . . . Instead of saying, "Lord, to-
> day I exaggerated a little on my expense account, but
> you know everyone does," I was able to say, "Lord I
> *cheated* on my expense account today. Help me not to
> be a dirty thief." Or instead of saying, "Lord, I couldn't
> help noticing that secretary down the hall . . . it was
> such a windy day . . . but Lord you know that boys will
> be boys," I began to be able to level with God and to
> say openly to him, "Lord, I thought of sleeping with
> that girl in my imagination. This is the kind of man I

am. Forgive me and give me the power and the desire to be different."[14]

We've talked about listening to others and sitting silently in communion with our friends, but we perhaps have not realized that prayer, too, "is a listening ear." Fosdick says that "one of our strongest misconceptions concerning prayer is that it consists chiefly in our *talking* to God, whereas the best part of prayer is our *listening* to God."[15]

> "For God alone my soul waits in silence, for my hope is from him" (Psalm 62:5).
> Be still, and know that I am God" (Psalm 46:10).
> Let me hear what God the Lord will speak, for he will speak peace to his people, to his saints, to those who turn to him in their hearts." (Psalm 85:8)

Have you met your Father and your God person to person? Do you know him as you know your child, your husband, your mother, your dearest friends? Before I visited Denver, I had read about the city, heard people talk about Denver, and had even seen pictures of Denver. But I had nothing of the feeling I have now, after having been there in person. And that surely is insignificant compared with the way those who live there know Denver, those who have loved the aspen quivering in the mountain breezes, the gaunt crags, the snow capped mountain peaks glistening in the sun, the rustle of leaves and bursts of autumn color. Similarly, do you know of God only what you have read, or is he real to you? When you pray, are you aware of the presence of a person? Are you aware that you are talking to someone? Do you think that when Jesus cried out in the garden, he was talking into space? I can see him down on the ground, perhaps even beating his fists, with great drops running down his face. As he cried out, "Let this cup pass from me," he was talking to somebody. He can be just as near, just as sure as the touch of your hand on mine.

Ultimately and finally we come back to the beginning point: adoration, loving God back. "In the school of adoration the soul learns why the approach to every other goal [has] left it restless."[16] A strange thing happens when we go and simply kneel or sit in thankfulness and comradeship with him, not asking for things, not crying for understanding, not pouring out our problems, but just enjoying him. Simply being with him brings the peace and calm and order that we need just as we find soothing and release by being with our friends. How truly does Fosdick say that "the great gift of God in prayer is himself, and whatever else he gives is incidental and secondary."[17]

> ... O glorious and blessed God, Father, Son and Holy Spirit, Thou art mine, and I am Thine. So be it.[18]

REFERENCES

REFERENCES

CHAPTER ONE—*TOUCHING WOUNDS*

[1]Bel Kaufman, *Up the Down Staircase* (Englewood Cliffs, N.J.: Prentice-Hall, Inc., 1964), p. 166.

[2]*Ibid.*, pp. 166-168, *passim.*

[3]*Ibid.*, p. 167.

[4]As quoted by Pat Harrell in "The Inner Closet, Widen Your Hearts," *Kerygma*, Vol. 1, No. 2 (1965), p. 43.

[5]Keith Miller, *The Taste of New Wine* (Waco, Texas: Word Books, 1965), p. 73.

[6]Philip Dunning, "Every Fellow Needs a Friend," *International Journal of Religious Education*, 34 (April, 1958), p. 10.

[7]Dietrich Bonhoeffer, *Life Together* (New York: Harper & Row, 1954), p. 93.

[8]Kaufman, *op. cit.*, p. 180.

[9]As quoted in Edna B. Trickey, "Beyond the Classroom," *International Journal of Religious Education* 41 (Sept., 1964), p. 10.

[10]Harry Emerson Fosdick, *The Meaning of Service* (New York: Association Press, 1950), p. 99.

[11]Eleanor Morrison and Virgil Foster, *Creative Teaching in the Church* (Englewood Cliffs, N.J.: Prentice-Hall, Inc., 1963), p. 21.

[12]Paul Tillich, *The New Being* (New York: Charles Scribner's Sons, 1955), p. 173.

[13]Paul Scherer, *The Interpreter's Bible*, George Buttrick, ed. (Nashville: Abingdon Press, 1952), Vol. 8, p. 390.

[14]Second Edition, Charles Scribner's Sons (New York, 1958), passim.

[15]W. Randolph Thornton, "Through Groups to God," *International Journal of Religious Education*, 33 (April, 1957), p. 5. Copyright 1957, Division of Christian Education, National Council of Churches. Used by permission.

CHAPTER TWO—*FAMILY GIVE AND TAKE*

[1]Havelock Ellis, *On Life and Sex* (New York: Doubleday and Doran, 1931), p. 19. Used by permission of Francoise

Delisle, copyright owner.

[2]*Ibid.*, p. 21.

[3]Harry and Bonaro Overstreet, "Building Sound Personality," *Childhood Education*, Vol. 32 (April, 1956), pp. 358-359.

[4]Paul Tournier, *Secrets*, trans. Joe Embry (Richmond, Va.: John Knox Press, 1965), p. 8.

[5]*Ibid.*, p. 19.

[6]*Ibid.*, pp. 20-21, *passim.*

[7]Nardi Reeder Campion, "Ask, Don't Tell," *Reader's Digest*, Vol. 89 (August, 1966), pp. 49-52, *passim.*

[8]Tournier, *op. cit.*, p. 29.

[9]Hermeline O'Sullivan, "Make Memories for Your Children."

[10]*Ibid.*

[11]Miller, *op. cit.*, p. 51.

[12]Tournier, *op. cit.*, pp. 45-56, *passim.*

[13]Ellis, *op. cit.*, p. 54.

[14]Olive Schreiner, in a personal letter. Quoted in Ellis, *loc. cit.*

[15]*Loc. cit.*, idea from Mrs. Havelock Ellis, *James Minton.*

[16]Guy de Maupassant, as quoted in Henry A. Bowman, *Marriage for Moderns* (New York: McGraw-Hill, 1965), p. 678.

[17]John S. Hoyland, from "A Prayer for Family Love," *Masterpieces of Religious Verse*, ed. James Dalton Morrison (New York: Harper & Brothers, 1948), p. 344.

CHAPTER THREE—*CHRISTIAN COMMUNITY*

[1]Winfred E. Garrison, *The Quest and Character of a United Church* (Nashville: Abingdon Press, 1957), p. 46.

[2]Bonhoeffer, *op. cit.*, p. 18.

[3]*Ibid.*, p. 20.

[4]Douglas V. Steere, "Prayer and Worship," *The Religous Life* (New York: Association Press, 1939), p. 37.

[5]Elton Trueblood, *The Company of the Committed* (New York: Harper & Brothers, 1961), p. 113.

[6]*Ibid.*, p. 96.

[7]Bonhoeffer, *op. cit.*, p. 101.

[8]Mary Lou Walden, in unpublished ms.

[9]Bonhoeffer, *op. cit.*, p. 99.

[10]Fosdick, *The Meaning of Service*, p. 45.

[11]*Ibid.*

[12]Bonhoeffer, *op. cit.*, p. 110.

[13]Miller, *op. cit.*, pp. 60-61.

[14]Bonhoeffer, *op. cit.*, pp. 112-118, *passim.*

[15]*Ibid.*, pp. 118-119, *passim.*

[16]Steere, *op. cit.*, p. 31.

[17]Trueblood, *op. cit.*, p. 75.

[18]Miller, *op. cit.*, p. 75.

[19]Gerald O. Young, "Breaking or Understanding?" *International Journal of Religious Education*, 41 (Nov. 1964), p. 3.

CHAPTER FOUR—*BEYOND THE CIRCLE*

[1]J. B. Phillips, *When God was Man* (Nashville: Abingdon Press, 1955), p. 34.

[2]Trueblood, *op. cit.*, p. 69.

[3]William H. Hollister, "The Church 'Out there,'" *International Journal of Religious Education*, 42 (Sept., 1965), pp. 4-5.

[4]Peter Marshall, "Gallery Christians," in *A Man Called Peter* by Catherine Marshall (New York: McGraw-Hill, 1951), pp. 302-303, *passim.*

[5]Hubert G. Locke, "The Church and Civil Rights," *Kerygma*, Vol I, No. 2 (1965), p. 7.

[6]John Howard Griffin, *Black Like Me* (Boston: Houghton Mifflin Co.) cited from the New American Library edition, 1961, p. 106.

[7]*Ibid.*, pp. 108-109.

[8]*Ibid.*, p. 110.

[9]Trueblood, *op. cit.*, p. 65.

[10]Vachel Lindsay, "The Leaden-Eyed," in *Selected Poems of Vachel Lindsay*, ed. Mark Harris (New York: The Macmillan Co., 1963), p. 141.

[11]Harry and Bonaro Overstreet, *The Mind Goes Forth* (New York: W. W. Norton & Co., Inc., 1956), pp. 136-137.

[12]David Goodman, *A Parents' Guide to the Emotional*

Needs of Children (New York: Hawthorn Books, Inc., 1959), pp. 98-99.

[13]John Reddy, "A Few True Friends," *Reader's Digest*, Vol. 88, No. 525 (Jan. 1966), pp. 128-132, *passim.*

[14]Fosdick, *The Meaning of Service*, p. 48.

[15]Miller, *op. cit.*, p. 64.

[16]A. Roy Eckardt, "Compassion" *The Christian Century* 72 (Nov. 16, 1955), p. 1328.

CHAPTER FIVE—*THE ALABASTER JAR*

[1]Erich Fromm, *The Art of Loving* (New York: Bantam Books, 1963), p. 20. Used by permission of Harper & Row.

[2]Steere, *op. cit.*, p. 19.

[3]Fosdick, *The Meaning of Prayer* (New York: Association Press, 1951), p. 63.

[4]Gladys Taber, *Another Path* (New York: J. P. Lippincott Co., 1963), pp. 12-13.

[5]*Ibid.*, pp. 14-15.

[6]This poem in various forms has been attributed to Mary Carolyn Davies.

CHAPTER SIX—*FRIENDSHIP WITH GOD*

[1]Martin Buber, *I and Thou* (New York: Scribner's) p. 82.

[2]Walter Russell Bowie, *The Master: A Life of Jesus Christ* (New York: Charles Scribner's Sons, 1958), pp. 132-133.

[3]*Ibid.*, pp. 326-327.

[4]Georgia Harkness, "Religious Living," *The Religious Life* (New York: Association Press, 1939), pp. 6-7.

[5]In this paragraph and those following I am indebted for general ideas concerning the life of Christ to Walter Russell Bowie, *op. cit.*, passim.

[6]*Ibid.*, p. 80.

[7]*Ibid.*, pp. 76-78, *passim.*

[8]G. Campbell Morgan, *The Practice of Prayer* (Westwood, N.J.: Fleming H. Revell, 1960), p. 35.

[9]Fosdick, *The Meaning of Prayer*, p. 26.

[10]*Ibid.*, p. 75.

[11]Tournier, *op. cit.*, pp. 57-63, *passim.*

[12]*Ibid.*, p. 60.

[13]Douglas Steere, *Dimensions of Prayer* (New York: Harper & Row, 1963), p. 44.

[14]Miller, *op. cit.*, p. 59.

[15]Fosdick, *The Meaning of Prayer*, p. 62.

[16]Steere, *Prayer and Worship*, p. 35.

[17]Fosdick, *The Meaning of Prayer*, p. 30.

[18]From *The Methodist Shorter Book of Offices*.